EXPERIENCE OVER STUFF

How to Live Free in a World that Wants to Clutter You Up

Genevieve Parker Hill

Copyright © 2020 Genevieve Parker Hill

All rights reserved.

ISBN: 979-8-6465399-6-1

Contents

Chapter One 5
Chapter Two 25
Chapter Three 41
Chapter Four 47
Chapter Five 63
Chapter Six 78
Chapter Seven 91
Chapter Eight 101
Chapter Nine 108
Chapter Ten 119
Acknowledgements 127
Resources 128
Appendix 129

Parker Hill

Chapter One

The Situation: The World Wants to Clutter You Up

In the fall of 2018, I sat in a small office of a gym in Kyiv, Ukraine as a sales consultant explained the pricing of a membership to me. I'm from the United States, but my family and I are nomads who frequently live for stints abroad. Our move to Kyiv would give me my first opportunity ever to endure a truly cold, solidly snowy winter. I sought out a lot of advice. I was scared.

I'd been advised that the best way to thrive through winter here was to join a gym. Normally I like to exercise outdoors, but again, winter.

As I looked at what the gym offered, I started to understand why joining a gym would transform my experience of winter. For starters, the gym had spa rooms of various nationalities: a Russian bath spa, a Roman bath, and a Finnish sauna. There was also a cinema in the gym. If you're watching a movie at the gym, are you burning more calories than if you watch a movie at home?

Up to this point, learning about this relax-o-gym was all part of a wonderfully foreign experience. And then the salesperson pointed to a paper in front of her showing multiple price points, and in a gentle Ukrainian accent, said "And this is the special price for our Black Friday sale."

Black Friday? As in the American term for the sales and shopping rush on the day after Thanksgiving? Yes, that Black Friday. And Thanksgiving hadn't even come yet. When it did, it wasn't much of a thing in Ukraine.

Apparently, while marking Thanksgiving on the fourth Thursday of November has stayed solidly American, the next day's tradition of big discounts has spread around the world. As I walked around Kyiv, I began noticing other signs in windows advertising Black Friday sales and specials.

Ridiculously, Black Friday has gone global, *leaving behind* the American holiday that gave birth to it, Thanksgiving. Black Friday, a celebration of consumer frenzy, is now more famous than its parent holiday, one that focuses around giving thanks and spending time with loved ones.

Black Friday's global infamy shows us that the world wants to clutter us up. Well, not the world exactly, not planet Earth. Forces outside of us conspire with something inside of each of us that makes us think more stuff will make us happier. And it does, for a moment. Acquiring. Accumulating. Collecting. These activities satisfy a primal need to feel secure, safe, and powerful.

When the future is uncertain, which it always is, a solid collection of useful, helpful, beautiful, and entertaining products is comforting. We need things to live well.

But owning too many things makes us unwell. I gave evidence for this in my book *Minimalist Living: Decluttering for Joy, Health, and Creativity*. But you don't need research right now. You can look to your own personal experience to prove that owning too many things makes us unwell in body, mind, and spirit.

Owning a lot of stuff means having to take care of it. It can be a full-time job. So, we need to hire someone to take care of our many things, or we need to rent a place to shelter our things. Hiring someone or renting a place costs money.

Experience Over Stuff

That's a fine way to spend money if you choose consciously to do so. However, it's not a fine way to spend if you need your money for other things, like getting out of debt, saving for the future, or investing in your education and growth. Spending beyond our budget to shelter or care for our possessions can lead to financial stress and take a toll on our health.

We also need to spend time to take care of our things - to purchase, clean, move, organize, maintain, and use our things. And then there is the end of the life cycle. We must properly dispose of our things. Again, spending time taking care of our things is not a bad way to spend time. But how much time is too much?

When we zoom out, is this how we envisioned our lives? Spending this much time or money or both to take care of our things? This much time shopping and organizing and cleaning? Or did we imagine a life with more freedom?

I envision a life with a lot of freedom. And yet, even as someone who has written a couple books on the topic of simple living, I find myself buying more and more. Every year, I buy a lot more than I need. I even buy some things I do not end up using, needing, or enjoying. So let's explore this topic together.

The quality of our mindset, narratives, beliefs, visualizations, ideas, and relational connections (and so many other parts connected to our interior lives) is limited only by what we can imagine. Therefore there is no limit on how good those parts of your life can get; there is no limit on their power to support the life you desire.

We are limitless. We can create in those areas – mindset, narratives, beliefs, visualizations, ideas, relationship connections, and many others – what we can imagine. So let's develop imaginations as expansive, robust, ambitious, and brave as we can. Let's stretch the limits of our imaginations like athletes training for the Olympics. Let's become champions of imagining. Let's go further, higher, faster.

Author Glennon Doyle asks "What is the truest, most beautiful story about your life that you can imagine?"[1]

Imagine that, and then make it even better.

If you picked this book up, I know your vision for your own life includes focusing on experience over stuff and being free. This is a beautiful vision. Let's make it happen. But before we can rise above a certain situation, we need to know what it is. We need to understand where we are so we can establish point A and get to point B.

The Clutter Numbers

Americans are big buyers. The American Marketing Association reported that U.S. retailers earned a record $7.9 billion on Black Friday in 2017.[2]

Where is all that stuff going? Most of it ends up in our homes, which then feel chaotic, become hard to keep clean, and become places where it's hard to find what we're looking for. We also put our things in off-site storage that we must pay for, to store items we promptly forget we own. And sadly, much of what we purchase ends up in landfills.

Lest you think I'm criticizing Americans while standing apart; I'll share that I too have purchased things I almost immediately discarded. I've paid for off-site storage, and I'm far from zero-waste living. Although I've made progress in

---

[1] https://www.marieforleo.com/2020/03/glennon-doyle-untamed

[2] https://www.ama.org/publications/eNewsletters/Marketing-News-Weekly/Pages/black-friday-2017-infographic.aspx

Experience Over Stuff

turning away from consumerism, I still have much to learn. The first step is to shine a light on where we are now, both as individuals and as part of a society.

Let's look at some more clutter numbers to illuminate things.

These 10 statistics on clutter appeared in a post[3] on Joshua Becker's site Becoming Minimalist.

1. There are 300,000 items in the average American home.[4]

2. The average size of the American home has nearly tripled in size over the past 50 years.[5]

3. 1 out of 10 Americans rent offsite storage—the fastest growing segment of the commercial real estate industry over the past four decades.[6]

4. There are 2.63 billion square feet of rentable self-storage space in the U.S, or 7.06 square feet per person.[7] That means, theoretically, self-storage space could fit the entire population of the country.

---

[3] https://www.becomingminimalist.com/clutter-stats/

[4] http://articles.latimes.com/2014/mar/21/health/la-he-keeping-stuff-20140322

[5] https://www.npr.org/templates/story/story.php?storyId=5525283

[6] https://www.nytimes.com/2009/09/06/magazine/06self-storage-t.html?em&_r=0

[7] https://www.sparefoot.com/self-storage/news/1432-self-storage-industry-statistics/

5. 3.1% of the world's children live in America, but they own 40% of the toys consumed globally.[8]

6. The average American woman owns 30 outfits—one for every day of the month. In 1930, that figure was nine.[9]

7. Our homes have more television sets than people.[10]

8. Americans spend more on shoes, jewelry, and watches ($100 billion) than on higher education.[11]

9. Over the course of our lifetime, we will spend a total of 3,680 hours or 153 days searching for misplaced items.[12]

10. Some reports indicate we consume twice as many material goods today as we did 50 years ago.[13]

It feels like clutter creeps into our homes by itself and multiplies in drawers, closets, cupboards, and garages.

And yet the truth is we bring or allow each item into our homes. We bring in much more than we carry out. We place

---

[8] https://www.uctv.tv/RelatedContent.aspx?RelatedID=301

[9] https://www.forbes.com/sites/emmajohnson/2015/01/15/the-real-cost-of-your-shopping-habits/#f3eb6861452d

[10] http://usatoday30.usatoday.com/life/television/news/2006-09-21-homes-tv_x.htm

[11] https://www.psychologytoday.com/intl/blog/sex-drugs-and-boredom/201207/do-americans-consume-too-much

[12] https://www.dailymail.co.uk/news/article-2117987/Lost-today-Misplaced-items-cost-minutes-day.html

[13] http://storyofstuff.org/wp-content/uploads/movies/scripts/Story%20of%20Stuff.pdf

a great deal of attention and care on what we bring in. Shopping, thanks to a culture of consumerism, seems like our mission as humans. It's the goal, the dream, the ideal pastime. Annie Leonard, in *The Story of Stuff*, says, "Our primary identity has become that of consumer, not mothers, teachers, farmers, but consumers."[14] Buying stuff brings excitement, new hope, fresh dreams, and imagined solutions to our most discouraging and embarrassing problems. It feels great for a short time.

Selling is Not Evil

Let me be clear: I don't villainize shopping, or even the advertising and marketing industries. As humans, we're always trying to persuade each other of the merits of a thing or an idea. That's a sort of sales and marketing. To lead is to influence. It's natural and not inherently problematic. We will always be selling things to each other—and even selling ideas and experiences. This book itself is my attempt to sell you on a lifestyle that emphasizes experiences and freedom over the consumerist culture that we, in developed countries, are steeped in from birth. Marketers are not the enemy. In fact, many people in marketing wholeheartedly believe in their product. As a business owner, I understand this belief. It is *meaningful* to have a product or service to stand behind. And so the "experience over stuff" lifestyle isn't about products *versus* services. I don't believe services are better than products, but I do think we must become awake to what is going on around us. Awareness is everything.

Later we'll go into some tactics marketers use that we can start to notice around us. But for now, think about how you can "sell" yourself on living simply to experience more freedom and joy.

---

[14] http://storyofstuff.org/wp-content/uploads/movies/scripts/Story%20of%20Stuff.pdf

Our Trash Problem

We humans have conquered the planet. There are 7.6 billion of us on Earth.[15] We are not yet close to overwhelming the planet's capacity, but our stuff may be. Each American creates an average of 4.5 pounds (just over 2 kilograms) of garbage per day.[16] And that's just what we throw out. Those who live in small homes and apartments don't have room to store many belongings. However, those who live in large homes or who rent off-site storage space may be unwittingly storing things bound for the trash.

One in ten people in the U.S. use self-storage. Again, there's nothing wrong with self-storage as a service, but it's a good measure of the fact that we will pay a monthly rental fee to *house* our stuff in a *separate* building. One that we are not in. And often, we find that a few short weeks or months later, we don't even remember what we put in storage. The things it seemed so important to keep that we would pay a thousand dollars a year or so to shelter, have been forgotten.

What we must realize is that if we are storing a lot of things that aren't being used, when we die, they will likely be thrown away. Sure, some things will be claimed by relatives or donated to charity, but the truth, to turn around the old saying, is *one person's treasure is junk to almost everyone else*. I wrote my book *Minimalist Living: Decluttering for Joy, Health, and Creativity*, partly inspired by my grandmother's story of seeing her antique-collecting neighbor's home emptied of its contents. After her neighbor passed away, her children threw everything into a large dumpster. My Gram's best guess was that this neighbor simply had so much clutter that her children felt that they

---

[15] https://population.io/

[16] https://www.exploringnature.org/db/view/Too-Much-Trash

couldn't deal with finding homes for the items. The treasures were lost amidst the trash.

Once your eyes are open to how much trash we make through our purchases – as well as to the statistics Josh Becker compiled, it's very hard to get them closed again.

A Simpler Life

It's time to find a new normal: a simpler life that we are happier with. To get there we must subtract. To stay there, we must not buy as much stuff. When we occasionally get carried away with shopping, as most of us do, we must go back to editing. So many things in life are improved with editing. Our homes and schedules are no exception.

We know this. We admire the clutter free, light-filled minimalist rooms featured on Instagram, home décor websites, and magazines. We feel a pang of irritation when our smart phones ping. We don't know which of the dozens of apps we've installed to improve our life is updating us with nonessential information. We long for simplicity and the contentment we imagine comes along with it.

And yet it is an uphill battle. None of us can completely avoid the never-ending tidal wave of marketing messages aimed at us. At least not without leaving civilization to live like a monk in a cave somewhere. And even then, we must be picky about the cave, as somewhere there a monk asking their fellow monk what the Wi-Fi password is.

Most of us are not going to give up our chosen lives and become minimalist monks. We try to apply simplicity to our lives as they are. But it's hard. Although we may host a weekend yard sale occasionally, we fight hard not to give in to the onslaught of stuff. And often we fail.

Shopping and Selling and Shopping Some More

Sometimes we have the sense that shopping is part of what makes us human, or at least, American. Anthropologist Dr. Peter G. Stromberg writes in *Psychology Today*, "Many of the most important rituals in American culture center around the consumption of goods and services: we buy a lot of stuff."[17]

Even when we travel, Americans are encouraged to shop. Years ago, I was reading a travel guidebook, and I was struck by how for every location discussed, the main activity listed, after some light sightseeing was, you guessed it, shopping.

Something else we know: shopping is often not in our best interest. However, we do not often talk about the delicate matter of how much we overspend. Tellingly, total credit card debt in the U.S. is now over 1 trillion USD. In early 2018, CNBC reported that the average household with credit card debt owes $16,883.[18]

Why is it so hard to stop over-shopping?

We live in a debt-friendly society that places cultural importance on shopping. It's helpful to know not just that, but also some behind-the-scenes details on what goes into selling you a new thing.

Advertising is geared to bypass the logical, most evolved part of our brain and to trigger fear and deep, primal needs like

---

[17] https://www.psychologytoday.com/intl/blog/sex-drugs-and-boredom/201207/do-americans-consume-too-much

[18] https://www.cnbc.com/2018/01/23/credit-card-debt-hits-record-high.html

Experience Over Stuff

the need to be safe, to fit in, and to be loved. We know we can't buy our way to love, but it doesn't stop us from trying.

A huge number of people in the U.S. are employed in selling us things. You might even be part of one of the industries that connects people to products. The industries that are responsible for selling include marketing, brand management and development, advertising, promotions, public relations, and media relations. That's a lot of industries. Vault.com reports, "In the United States, the marketing consultant industry is a 43 billion dollar business, consisting of nearly 198,000 businesses that employed more than 355,000 workers in 2016, as reported by the market research group IBISWorld."[19] And that number doesn't include people for whom marketing is part of a broader job description.

There's a magnitude to the forces that come together to clutter us up. These forces are bigger than you and me. It's best to know what we're up against.

Corporations spend massive amounts of money to get your eyes on their stuff. Walmart, the largest company in the world according to Fortune.com,[20] spends an estimated 3.1 billion USD per year on advertising alone.[21] That's just one company.

Within the sphere of advertising, it's hardly a matter of companies throwing money at advertising firms, hoping what they come up with sells products by luck or chance. Rigorous research goes toward digging into our psychology

---

[19] http://www.vault.com/industries-professions/industries/marketing.aspx

[20] http://fortune.com/global500/

[21] https://www.statista.com/statistics/622029/walmart-ad-spend/

as consumers. The Journal of Consumer Psychology[22] publishes papers with titles like "The Ties That Bind: Measuring the Strength of Consumers' Emotional Attachments to Brands" and "How Financial Constraints Influence Consumer Behavior: An Integrative Framework."

Did you know that if you have an unrequited romantic crush, you are more likely to try new products? That's what the authors of a paper entitled "Romantic Crushes Support Variety-Seeking Behavior" theorize.[23] They write, "we suggest that the lack of reciprocal response in the romantic crush experience may lower consumers' sense of control in the romantic relationship. Therefore, they are motivated to restore their sense of control by making more varied choices in consumption domains. Five studies provide support for this hypothesis."

Spending on marketing goes well beyond advertising and research. It also includes the routine activities of packaging, cleaning, and window-styling products. Innumerable employee hours go towards the goal of making a product appealing enough to catch our attention and get us to open our wallets.

Our country is about selling and buying. Businesses are financially rewarded for making products people want and offering valuable services. Our capitalist economy is built on it. This is not a problem, at least, not one of our main problems as I see it.

What I would like us to do is go into every shopping experience with more *awareness*. We can't change what's

---

22

https://onlinelibrary.wiley.com/doi/abs/10.1207/s15327663jcp1501_10

23

https://onlinelibrary.wiley.com/doi/full/10.1002/jcpy.1070

out there; we must change what's inside, in our minds and hearts. We have to seize control of our internal focus. And the first step to a new awareness is seeing that from the moment we step outside our homes, and often before, we are shopping.

When we watch television or YouTube videos, we watch ads, and that is part of shopping. When we pick up our smart phone to look up an article or check a fact, we'll likely see an ad. That is the beginning of shopping.

So, shopping starts at home.

And then we leave our homes and see advertising all over our towns and cities.

Then we talk to our friends and coworkers. In the book *Contagious: Why Things Catch On*,[24] Jonah Berger posits that word-of-mouth is a powerful force influencing something to go viral. "People share more than 16,000 words per day and every hour there are more than 100 million conversations about brands," he writes. We are swayed by what the people around us are doing and talking about. "The things others tell us, email us, and text us have a significant impact on what we think, read, buy, and do. [...] Word of mouth is the primary factor behind 20 to 50 percent of all purchasing decisions."

So, not only must we be aware of our own tendency to be manipulated by marketing messages, but we must pay special attention to our family, friends, and coworkers purchasing habits, because they influence us.

---

[24] A link to this book and all other recommended books mentioned within these pages can be found at: https://simplelivingtoolkit.com/blog/experiencebooks

Marketing Tactics to Notice

How do you live free in a world that wants to clutter you up?

"I don't watch a lot of TV anymore because of the commercials that say you need this or that. I make myself more aware of the tactics they use as well. I try to spend more time doing other things, like running or hiking with my favorite kids."

—Rachel Matthews via the Minimalist Living Facebook page[25]

Like Rachel, I don't watch a lot of TV. Even though I miss out on those annoying commercials, I still see advertising everywhere. Let's look at some of the tactics advertisers use on us – not necessarily to avoid making purchases, but to avoid making purchases for the wrong reasons.

In the book I mentioned above, *Contagious: Why Things Catch On*, the author presents the research on what elements make a piece of advertising content more likely to go viral. Berger gives an acronym, STEPPS that helps the key concepts stick in the reader's mind. I'll summarize the first three (STE) concepts here because they are widely used tactics to notice as you learn to open your eyes to the commercial content you see in your daily life. If you want to learn the last three tactics, I recommend reading Berger's book.

The first "S" stands for social currency. Basically, advertisers want to tap into our human desire to seem cool, popular, or

---

[25] This and following comments cited from the Minimalist Living Facebook page can be found here: https://www.facebook.com/mnmlstlvng/photos/a.55808815 7608454.1073741825.383625691721369/1528052713945322 /?type=3&theater with a screenshot in the Appendix.

on-trend. If we think a product or a story related to a product will make us seem like we are part of an elite group, we are more likely to buy it or talk about it.

The "T" stands for "Triggers" which refers to the way we connect ideas. For example, in America, we connect "peanut butter" with "jelly" because of the popularity of peanut butter and jelly sandwiches. Peanut butter marketers will use jelly to get you to think of peanut butter and vice versa. Look for obvious cues (like peanut butter and jelly) and subtle cues in advertising messages.

The "E" stands for emotions. Advertisers play on our emotions like a fiddle, especially what Berger calls "arousal" emotions, which include awe, excitement, delight, surprise, anger, outrage, and anxiety. I don't mind when a commercial message influences me to feel awe or delight, but I do take issue with those meant to inspire fear or anxiety. A lot of advertisements do this, subtly or overtly. Keep an eye out for these fear-based advertisements, especially in the beauty industry.

Now you know a few marketing strategies to notice. Reflection is vital. We are almost constantly bombarded with marketing messages. They aren't negative in themselves, but when we allow them to bypass our logical reasoning brain, they can influence us to clutter up our lives with things we don't need and that we don't really want.

What do we actually want? We want the emotions we *think* the purchase will give us. These feelings are essential. Positive emotions are a sign that our needs are met, while negative emotions mean our needs are *not* met or may be in danger of not being met. Once we can identify the needs behind the feelings, we are well on our way to having a variety of options at our fingertips that will inspire more positive feelings. We can choose tactics that don't involve buying a thing we don't need. This requires true presence to our feelings and corresponding needs.

Core Human Needs

Some basic humans needs we all have (beyond survival needs for food and shelter) according to Marshall B. Rosenberg's book *Being Me, Loving You*, are:

- Autonomy
- Celebrating
- Mourning
- Integrity
- Interdependence
- Physical nurturance
- Sexual expression
- Rest
- Play
- Spiritual Communion

Knowing how we feel and what the need behind our emotions are can help us when it comes to living an aware, conscious life and avoiding falling prey to impulse purchases. Usually when that happens it's because we are believing "this thing is the *only* thing that will make me feel _____ and which meets my need for _____." That's always a lie. The wonderful, bountiful thing about life is there are many ways to meet individual needs. There is never only one way.

According to Nonviolent Communication, we can most effectively communicate with the people around us when we express our emotions and needs with clear requests which don't use words that judge or criticize. When we think and speak in language that directly communicates our own feelings and needs at the appropriate time, we are more likely to get our needs met.

Not There Yet

How do you live free in a world that wants to clutter you up?

"Not there yet, so reading and joining groups to help me see a clutter free future."

—Julie Duchesne via the Minimalist Living Facebook page

Not there yet. Me neither. This is a process. Many people use the term "minimalism journey" because this work does feel like one long journey out of consumerism and into a lighter, more free way of living. Let's take it one baby step at a time.

More than A Moment

We are fighting back against the urge to clutter up our homes and lives. Whether you call yourself a minimalist or have merely a pop-culture-based interest in Marie Kondo's *The Life-Changing Magic of Tidying Up*, whether you want to travel the world with only a backpack or you just want to be able to see what you have in your closet or kitchen cabinet, you are fighting back just by starting here. By reading this book. And you're part of a global movement.

It's in full swing in the US. And it's catching on all over the world. An article titled "Less is more: Why affluent Indians are going minimalist" in the *India Economic Times* details the rise of minimalism in India and touches on the movements in Japan and Scandinavia.[26]

The experience over stuff movement is gaining power. It's here to stay. This is more than a moment; it's a movement.

---

[26] https://economictimes.indiatimes.com/magazines/panache/less-is-more-why-affluent-indians-are-going-minimalist/articleshow/66101820.cms

Multi-Generational Minimalism

Minimalism is embraced by people of all generations, but the largest group in the U.S. currently embracing experience over stuff might be millennials. Writing for Forbes, Deborah Weinswig shares, "Millennials have a unique set of values around how they choose to spend their money. They grew up during the recession, entered a struggling job market and must now pay off record amounts of student debt." She quotes retail expert Robin Lewis, who says, "This is a generation that is bigger than the boomers in population, but their wallets are smaller, and they are more into the style of life than the stuff of life." Weinswig continues, "They prefer to spend on experiences rather than on stuff. Seventy-eight percent of millennials—compared to 59% of baby boomers—'would rather pay for an experience than material goods,' according to a survey from Harris Poll and Eventbrite cited on Bloomberg."[27]

While millennials may be embracing "the style of life" over "the stuff of life," all generations are putting their own spin on simple living and minimalism. Later we'll talk about retirees who are choosing the adventure life over the armchair life – and spending less in the process. The joys of simple living are for everyone, no matter their age. The older we get, the more possessions we tend to accumulate, and sometimes we hit a certain point, and get a wakeup call about how we want our home and environment to feel. Minimalist living can bring value to your life whatever your age may be. It's a movement for all.

27

https://www.forbes.com/sites/deborahweinswig/2016/09/07/millennials-go-minimal-the-decluttering-lifestyle-trend-that-is-taking-over/#56965b7c3755

With a New Mindset, It's Less of a Battle

In late 2017 I was on a computer refreshing the Amazon listing for my book. The title, *Minimalist Living: Decluttering for Joy, Health, and Creativity*, wasn't new, having been published years ago in 2013, but it strikes a nerve to this day. It became reading material for a growing movement of Americans – and people from many other countries – ending their love affair with stuff and embracing minimalism or "simple living."

Now it was time to watch the results of a promotional push for the book and we were not disappointed. My husband and I watched as it hit #1 in the "Sustainable Living" category and stayed on the Amazon Category best seller lists for days.

It's only just getting started, this minimalism movement. And it finds its real power when people see it as more than a trend that helps them get organized and clear out some closet space. It finds its power when we take it on as a mindset. When experience over stuff is my attitude, keeping my home and life simpler becomes less of a battle.

That's a good thing, because the exciting part about this movement is reclaiming joy. It shouldn't be a battle to be present and enjoy your life. The new mindset is based on fully inhabiting – from the heart – each moment in your life, not just dreaming about the happiness you might find in a new possession.

Experience over stuff is about defining, for yourself, what values, experiences, and emotions you want to have in your life. Then you design that life and choose it – whether it looks conventional or unconventional – around those experiences you desire.

My first two simple living books were about working from the outside in. Making your environment conducive to your joy. This book is more about working from the inside out – it's about the interplay between your interior life and your environment. It's about how to center your life more fully on the purposeful, meaningful, energizing activities that bring you steady joy. It's also learning that pain is always going to part of our human experience. Pain is part of life. How we respond to our own pain is one of the most important choices we each make.

And so, while we know that great relationships contribute to our happiness, the relationship we'll start with is the one you have with yourself. Once you learn to be yourself and accept yourself, pain and all, you're ready to experience deeper, healthier, more joyful relationships with the people in your life, the activities you participate in, and with the belongings you choose to have in your environment.

In her book *Untamed*, activist Glennon Doyle writes, "Consumer culture promises us that we can buy our way out of pain – that the reason we're sad and angry is not that being human hurts; it's because we don't have those countertops, her thighs, these jeans. This is a clever way to run an economy but it is no way to run a life. Consuming keeps up distracted, busy, and numb. Numbness keeps up from becoming."

It is time to become.

It is time to become yourself.

Chapter Two

The Solution: Being Yourself

Let's roll back through the years to my childhood for a moment.

After being homeschooled for a decade, I enrolled in public school for the first time. I would be attending a high school with 2,000 other students, a far cry from what I was used to – sharing a kitchen classroom with my three siblings.

I was a sheltered kid. No drugs, sex, and very little rock and roll had been part of my life up to that point. I walked the halls of my new school feeling shy and deeply self-conscious. I hugged my textbooks to my chest and gave myself the social-life-improving challenge of trying to make eye contact with someone. Anyone.

Thankfully, that first semester, in one of my classes, I was seated next to Jewel. She was as extroverted as I was introverted. Jewel greeted me with a megawatt smile every day and would happily yell my name in greeting down the hallways when she happened to see me getting jostled along on the way to my next class.

One day, arriving in the classroom, she threw herself into the chair next to me and ostentatiously rifled through the contents of her purse, allowing some of them to spill onto her desk.

A pack of cigarettes tumbled out. She looked at me with a grin before stuffing them back in her handbag.

"Jewel, I didn't know you smoked," I said, scandalized.

Jewel's grin grew wider, before she whispered conspiratorially, "I don't."

"Then why...?" I pointed to the cigarettes still visible in her open bag.

"I put them in there so my boyfriend finds them. And when he does, he's going to get mad. He doesn't want me to smoke."

"Okay?"

"So, he'll be mad, and we'll have a fight."

I was really confused.

"And you want to fight?"

"Yes," Jewel said, as if there was something clear that I wasn't getting. "Because then we'll have... make up sex."

Jewel sighed and leaned back with a dreamy smile. Class was about to start.

Wow, I thought. Make up sex must be the best if it's worth this elaborate ruse.

To this day, I don't know what to make of this interaction with Jewel. I am still really confused. I have so many questions.

Did I misunderstand her? Was she just covering for the fact that she smoked and didn't want me to judge her for it? Had she, at age 16, really had so much sex as to arrive at a clear preference for one type, and was it necessary to stage a reason to argue with her boyfriend to get it? Also, what kind of boyfriend routinely, predictably snooped around in his girlfriend's bag?

My point in sharing this odd tale of adolescent confusion is that teenagers, whether extroverted like Jewel, or introverted like me, don't know who they are or how to communicate clearly. They're still figuring it out. I couldn't read Jewel's true intentions. And Jewel, for her part, was still figuring out the best way to get what she wanted out of a romantic relationship.

The best way to make friends, they say, is to *be yourself*. I'm sure more than one person told me that when I was a lonely teen trying to make friends in high school.

But you must know and accept yourself to present your true self to the world. That's what "being yourself" means. And it takes time to know yourself. It takes time, experience, courage, honesty, and compassion to accept yourself.

Many adults I know are still figuring out self-knowledge and self-acceptance, me included. A teenager who knows herself, even a little, is way ahead of the game and she should be commended and encouraged on this path.

When it comes to living a life of freedom and joy, a life of experience over stuff, being yourself is important.

Being yourself is the secret.

How do you live free in a world that wants to clutter you up?

"'When you are content to be simply yourself and don't compare or compete, everybody will respect you.' (Lao Tzu) I keep this wisdom in mind... especially comparing. Not comparing lets me live free! "

–Gail Roesinger via the Minimalist Living Facebook page

Just be yourself.

It's the hardest advice in the world to follow. Don't follow the herd. Don't buy something to keep up with the Joneses or the Kardashians. Don't do something just because someone asked you to or because you're afraid you'll be missing out if you don't.

How do you live free in a world that wants to clutter you up?

"Let GO of all the things you thought you were supposed to be and just be the YOU, you were meant to be all along."

–Melissa Schmidt via the Minimalist Living Facebook page

If you follow your true north, you're much more likely to build a life of freedom and joy than if you keep switching directions based on outside trends and whims.

Being Yourself is Hard

"I contain multitudes." – Walt Whitman, "Song of Myself"

Those multitudes Walt Whitman mentions are what make being yourself a tall order.

There's the me that wants to eat more chocolate cake and the me that wants to go hiking and the me that wants to write this book. There's the me of my imagination, my dreams, and my fears, and then there's the me that is defined by my actions.

Then there's growth. We are always changing and growing. The more uncomfortable things get, the more apt we are to shift and stretch our ideas of who we are and what we are capable of. As the titular character (played by Will Smith) in the 2005 movie *Hitch* says, "*You* is a very fluid concept right now."

And yet. There's something true and real and unique within all of us. Call it our higher power, inner voice, God, a piece of heaven, or just our best selves. It's what's inside us that gives us our ability to be unique and, paradoxically, to connect to others.

That is the you I'm referring to when I say the answer is to be yourself.

So how do we identify our true, best selves, and live from there? And how do we differentiate *that* us from the fearful voices that don't have our best interests at heart?

It takes courage, for starters. Being yourself takes a strong heart. Because there is only one you. That means that being yourself will lack the easy comfort of following exactly what someone else is doing.

Being yourself is the ultimate grown up act. We spend our childhoods learning who we are as reflected in those around us, our adolescents fighting between a desire to fit in and a desire to continue to discover and express who we are, and then, hopefully, we really grow up.

Being yourself requires standing behind your convictions with courage and changing them when you realize your beliefs were wrong. It takes courage both to stand strong and to change and grow. Being yourself, first of all, requires honesty with yourself.

That can be hard. We must face what is real about us, even if we don't like it.

The other day, I had a conversation with my partner that left me feeling frozen. He was talking about his goals and our shared vision for the future. And then he said something that made it feel like winter was rolling ice down my spine.

I felt instantly in pain and angry. I knew that logically what he said wasn't unkind or unreasonable. I also knew if I opened my mouth, I'd say something hurtful and angry. So I shut down. I said nothing. We went to bed. The next day the pain I felt had gone into my body. I did the minimum I needed to do to take care of the kids and spent the rest of the day in bed, nursing my aching stomach. He checked in on me, wanting to talk. I could not bear to speak, couldn't explain what was going on. Finally, that night, after we'd tucked in the kids, I was ready to talk. We tried our best to understand each other. I cried a lot. I lay down on the floor. He peeled me off the floor and gave me a hug.

This is who I am. I'm intense. I somaticize. This is who I am right now, and I accept this experience.

"I am not a human being enjoying a spiritual life. I am a spiritual being enjoying a human life," wrote Pierre Teilhard de Chardin in *The Phenomenon of Man*.[28]

To embrace our true selves is to embrace the experience we're having right now as spiritual beings. *To integrate the spiritual with the human with compassionate understanding.* It's a life's work to do so. There are many ways to approach this journey.

However, there are time-tested practices that help us discover and own our authentic selves. Here are a few.

Meditation

How do you live free in a world that wants to clutter you up?
"Meditation."

–Erich Kulibert via the Minimalist Living Facebook page.

Meditation is a simple practice that requires nothing except yourself and some quiet time. The benefits can be immense. One overview of scientific studies appearing on Healthline cited at least ten evidence-backed health benefits of

---

[28] https://www.goodreads.com/work/quotes/1017318-le-ph-nom-ne-humain

meditation.[29] Some of these benefits include reducing stress, controlling anxiety, promoting emotional health, and enhancing self-awareness.

Leo Babauta of *Zen Habits* writes, "some of the best benefits of meditation are hard to define — you begin to understand yourself better, for example, and form a self-awareness level you've never had before." He claims that the habit of meditation is one of the most powerful things he's ever learned.[30]

Presence

The simple mission of meditation is to maintain presence. Our minds are busy, cluttered places – at least mine is – before meditating. A practice of mindful meditation has us first focus on observing our breathing. When the mind wanders to other thoughts, we simply observe that without judgment. Then, with gentleness and compassion, we bring our focus back to our breath.

This practice during meditation teaches us to be more present during all our daily activities. It trains the mind to find peace and focus more quickly. It shows us how to handle obsessive, irritating, or anxious thoughts when they come throughout the day – by returning to the present.

This practice also shows us the beginning of acceptance. For if we are to be fully here and present, we must accept this moment and everything that is happening now.

In *Practicing the Power of Now: Essential Teachings, Meditations, and Exercises from the Power of Now,* Eckhart Tolle writes, "All you really need to do is accept this moment

---

[29] https://www.healthline.com/nutrition/12-benefits-of-meditation#section10

[30] https://zenhabits.net/meditate/

fully. You are then at ease in the here and now and at ease with yourself."[31]

Presence helps us avoid regret and experience the beautiful moments none of us want to miss. Author Kate Northrup shared a story on her podcast. In an episode titled "How to Expand Time,"[32] she related some written advice her mother, Christiane Northrup, gave her as part of a baby shower before the birth of Kate's second daughter. "They say that this time goes so fast; they say you're going to miss this time," her mother wrote, "but if you really take it in, you'll really experience it, and you won't have to miss it."

Reflecting on Purpose

Imagine waking up on a vacation day or a holiday. You can't wait to get up. You feel excited to do what you want to do – what you've chosen to do – with a sense of wonder and joy – not a sense of dread. How many days of your normal life do you experience like this?

Maybe for you it's most of your days. Maybe it's very few. But part of the goal of this book is to help you bring more positive emotions to your days, as well as acceptance of your negative emotions.

This comes from reflection. From asking yourself what you are meant to do and be – what your purpose is – and how you can move closer to that every day.

Reflection on what we want usually lands on values. Ultimately, we can't predict what every day will look like or what activities we will do. I've done enough "ideal day"

---

[31] https://www.goodreads.com/work/quotes/3437032-practicing-the-power-of-now-essential-teachings-meditations-and-exerc

[32] https://katenorthrup.com/podcast/episode-105-how-to-expand-time/

journaling exercises to know that I don't have just one ideal day. What might be ideal for one day would become boring after 500 days. Instead of saying "I'd like to do this," you begin to think, "I'd like to be _____." You fill in the blank with values like "grateful," "kind," "curious," "brave" or "creative."

When you dig deep enough into your values, you land on your "why," or your purpose. What do your values lead you to? What is the most important thing to you? Now you're ready to go back to what you want to create in your life and what you want to contribute.

The key, when building a bridge between the life you really want and what is happening, is to start with one tiny goal and then take baby steps in the right direction. My wise mom says something I'll paraphrase to, "the deeper the hole, the smaller the goal." The more emotionally low your feel, or the further from your goal you are, the more you should mentally mince. Occasionally it is possible and advisable to make massive, sudden changes, but usually not. Set about creating your vision with small, but important steps.

To figure out what is the next important thing to do, ask yourself what Gary Keller, in his book *The One Thing*, calls "the focusing question:" "What's the ONE Thing I can do today such that by doing it everything else will be easier or unnecessary?" Some people will be hugely inspired by that question, while others will want to run and hide. If you're in the latter camp, just ignore the question and move in the right general direction.

The Upside of Disaster

If you have trouble envisioning what makes your own life feel deeply meaningful or authentic, try imagining disaster or death. Though it may seem dramatic or morbid, it's a powerful tool.

In a blog post entitled, "Disasters force us to reconsider the importance of belongings"[33]
Katherine Martinko writes, "When fire, flood, or fierce winds are barreling toward your home, it is striking how material possessions cease to matter. Items that were once prized belongings are left behind without a second thought because the most important thing is escaping unscathed. When it comes down to those frantic last-minute decisions, people, pets, and photographs are pretty much all that matters." The article referenced a *Washington Post* piece titled, "'I could live simpler': Floods and Fires Make Americans rethink their love affair with stuff."[34]

My own journey into the experience over stuff lifestyle began when a fire ripped through my family's home while I was away traveling. Before the fire destroyed most of my belongings, I was a collector. I had trouble letting go of things. It's still not easy for me, but one quick remembrance of the fire, and it all comes back to me: not sadness over losing my things, but tremendous awe, joy, and gratitude that my family escaped with their lives. These feelings immediately remind me of my values. What's important to me are my people. My relationships.

Before the fire, I held onto things because I thought they defined me. I was afraid that without my collection of journals and postcards and shoes, I would forget who I was or be unable to communicate the truth of who I was with

---

[33] https://www.treehugger.com/green-home/disasters-force-us-reconsider-importance-belongings.html

[34] https://www.washingtonpost.com/lifestyle/i-could-live-simpler-floods-and-fires-make-americans-rethink-their-love-affair-with-stuff/2017/10/25/2e41ad2a-b4d9-11e7-a908-a3470754bbb9_story.html?utm_term=.868919ea9509#comments

Experience Over Stuff

others. Now I feel free to be my true self – the one I wake up with – every day. I don't need reminders about who I am. I am the same person with or without my stuff. The exterior trappings of my life do not make me who I am. Instead, my values, intentions, words, and actions define me.

Hopefully you are lucky enough not to have had your home burn down. Obviously, disasters and losses are painful and not something to wish for. However, they do illuminate what's truly important. Rumi wrote, "These pains you feel are messengers. Listen to them."[35]

One commenter wrote on minimalist Joshua Becker's blog: "When it's all gone, you won't remember it. Home is where my people are."[36] The writer had lost most of his belongings in the 2017 Tubbs fire in Santa Rosa, California.

If you're an imaginative person, it may help you to visualize what would happen if your stuff were destroyed in a sudden blaze or flood. How would you feel? What would you value? What would stand out as most important to you? If you're like most people, you'd be grateful to escape with your life and your family.

Imagining your own death is another tool that can unearth hints about what you really value and how you want to live out your time on earth.

The concept of looking death straight in the eye to feel more fully alive is addressed in Mark Manson's book *The Subtle Art of Not Giving a F*ck*. In the book's final section, he vividly describes approaching the edge of a cliff – one with a

---

[35] https://www.goodreads.com/work/quotes/965212-essential-rumi

[36] https://twitter.com/joshua_becker/status/920340966418014208

drop off that would unquestionably kill him were he to go over – as a powerfully life affirming experience. That's something not all of us need or want to do. I am personally not an adrenaline junkie. I can get just about the same sense of renewed meaning in my life by imagining a near death experience. Whether thinking about it makes you shudder or inspires you to live your best life, the truth is, we're all going to die.

It's funny that imagining disaster and death can get us focused on what good we want to create and what is most important about *life*. And, just to be clear, I'm not talking about anxiety loops or obsessive worry about bad things happening to us. I'm talking about a conscious use of reflecting on disaster or death to get us quickly, directly in touch with what is really, truly important. Try it and see what comes into focus for you.

Intentional Living

You've meditated for the emotional, spiritual, and health benefits. You've reflected on the life you really want, including the values you live from and how a disaster would clarify your values. So, what's the next puzzle piece to being yourself in a world that wants to clutter you up? Intentional living. It's where you implement your values. It's not easy, but it's worth it.

Blogger Lisa Avellan writes, "What I do matters. And if it matters, if I matter, then I am worth more than a life that just reacts to circumstance. Intentional living defines your life before circumstances destroy it." She writes that intentional living "assigns meaning to the moment before we lose anymore moments to the meaningless.[37]"

Intentional living requires that we do our best to live out our values. This can bring a depth and meaning to our daily

---

[37] http://simpleandsoul.com/intentional-living/

actions. So much of enjoying life is the story we tell ourselves about what is happening right now. Intentional living shapes that story as we attempt to consciously live what we believe.

Take the parenting chore of changing a diaper as an example. We can see it has just another mundane or unpleasant moment to get through, or we can change the story through intentional living. If one of our values is to be a present and nurturing parent or caregiver, then the simple act of changing a diaper is elevated to a primary way of living out that intention. Assigning our own meaning, such as considering how changing a diaper fulfils our values of being caring or nurturing, enriches the experience. Your thoughtful, joyful changing of the diaper sends out love for your child and into the world. You get to receive peace. You get to create grace and love. That's intentional living.

Likewise, intentional living means avoiding or ceasing those actions that do not align with our values.

Despite our best intentions, many of us end up, well, not living intentionally. We buy things we don't need or really want. We say yes to commitments for the wrong reasons – because it's easier than saying no, or because we don't want to disappoint the person asking us for our time. It takes courage to resist social pressure and NOT do what might seem polite and appropriate.

Filter questions are the antidote to our less-than-intentional reactions. We all have many filters tuned to a variety of settings. It's one of the reasons that it's so hard to live by our true inner voices. We have a filter that keeps us from saying hurtful things to our friends. That same filter – the one responsible for us not wanting to hurt our friends, can also lead us to want to please people, even at cost to our deepest held values.

Filter questions take what is normally an unconscious sifting process and make it conscious. We pause before we buy something or commit ourselves to an event or task. The pause is very important. It can feel uncomfortable, but it's vital because it gives us time to apply filter questions, which can feel unnatural when they are new.

Think of your own filter questions. They will reflect that which is most important to you. I recommend taking some time to think or write various possibilities down. Reflect on your filter questions and then rework them if necessary.

Because we all have limited time, we should have a limited number of filter questions. Somewhere in the realm of 3-5 is a good number to aim for. And they should reflect your top 3-5 values or priorities. For example, if one of your values is nurturing your family, one of your filter questions could be "Does this nurture my family?" And if it doesn't, it's a no. Unless it's a yes for one of your other filter questions. The more specific you can make them, the more helpful they will be.

As you consider what your filter questions are, conflicting values may come up. That's normal. Intentional living is supposed to help you get clear on your values. Watch out for unexamined values that may come from someone else, such as an authority figure from your childhood. Every value you live by should be something you are aware of and can own as yours. Hidden, unclaimed, or unexamined values are the ones that cause problems.

Prayer and the Power of Group Intention

Prayer is another way to bring intentional living into your life. In fact, "intentions" is another word for "prayers." So you could call "intentional living," "prayerful living," if that suits you.

Prayer is an important part of every religion I have ever studied. The power of prayer, and especially its positive impact on the person doing the praying, is the topic of many religious texts and scriptures. But it's not only faith traditions that bear witness to the power of prayer.

The book *The Power of Eight*, by Lynne McTaggart, lays out compelling evidence that when people gather in a group of eight or so, their shared intention gets a power boost. Even when the group selflessly prays for someone outside the circle – as long as they are all holding the same shared intention – the group members benefit as well. While the person being prayed for often benefitted, the intenders did too. The individuals forming the prayer group experienced improved health and relationships, and even some miraculous healings. Interestingly, this kind of prayer may have been something Jesus taught his disciples, who prayed together "with one accord" in Acts 1:14.

Seeking Meaning

Being yourself is the ultimate act of honesty. It can feel vulnerable. Honesty with ourselves means we accept all the things about ourselves – even the imperfect things. The more authentically we can live, the higher quality our life experience.

But does being yourself mean never changing? No, we are all constantly changing and growing. Our desires and dreams can change too. Most of us want, first, to survive, to be safe and healthy, and then once those needs are met, we seek happiness and fulfillment through creation, contribution, and connection.

We want experiences that make us feel happy, joyful, and energized. But we won't stop with merely pleasurable experiences. We want to feel all the emotions. We want to feel fully alive. We want to build life of purpose. We want a life that's meaningful.

The meaning we find – and make - turns sacrifices and pain towards a greater purpose. When life seems devoid of meaning, things can quickly take a turn towards the dark and depressing. But when we find meaning, we can survive – and maybe even thrive - through almost anything.

CHAPTER THREE

OUR SEARCH FOR MEANING

While Regina Lark was earning a doctorate in history, she needed books. A lot of books. By the time she was finished with the degree, the volumes she'd collected filled her bookcases.

When it was time to pare down before a move to an apartment, Lark decided that the books meant something. They represented her accomplishment and intelligence, she thought.[38]

But did they really?

She began to ask herself some questions: "Who am I without these books? What will people think of me? Getting rid of them, am I less smart?"

She concluded that it was okay to let the books go, and she found satisfaction in donating them to another doctoral student.

Many people don't ask the questions Regina Lark asked about her books. Many people assume that it is objects that give their lives meaning. They believe that things represent who they are.

---

[38] http://articles.latimes.com/2014/mar/21/health/la-he-keeping-stuff-20140322

I used to be like that. But when you ask yourself questions like "who would I be without this item?" Or when you find yourself suddenly robbed of your things, you realize that you would be exactly who you are with or without the thing.

We are free to seek meaning outside of our material possessions and inside ourselves.

Where we look for meaning can deeply affect our mindset and quality of life.

Meaning in a Death Camp

In the book *Man's Search for Meaning*, Viktor Frankl wrote about his time as a prisoner in a Nazi death camp during World War Two. He observed, through his own psychoanalyst's perspective, differences in how the prisoners around him held onto hope despite unimaginable suffering. He noticed the ones who were able to will themselves to live another day despite the horrors of the concentration camp, seemed to have found a deep sense of purpose or meaning worth living for. Those who lost a sense of meaning found their bodies weakening. Death quickly followed in the merciless and dehumanizing conditions of the concentration camp. He wrote, "Everything can be taken from a man but one thing: the last of the human freedoms—to choose one's attitude in any given set of circumstances, to choose one's own way."[39]

Frankl himself held onto a vision of what made his life meaningful in two ways. He had many imaginary conversations with his beloved wife who was taken to another camp. Even though he was not able to see her or even find out if she was still alive, remembering the power of the *love* they shared helped him remember who he was and

---

[39] https://www.goodreads.com/work/quotes/3389674-trotzdem-ja-zum-leben-sagen-ein-psychologe-erlebt-das-konzentrationslag

what made life meaningful. Secondly, he envisioned a purpose his life could have if he survived the camp. He envisioned himself helping many people through speeches he would give about psychology and what he'd learned during his time as a prisoner.

If you could put yourself in Frankl's shoes, what do you think would have helped you get through one of the most dehumanizing and horrific experiences we can imagine? What meaningful vision would keep you going?

What's Meaningful to You?

Your meaning may not be my meaning. We each have to find our own. But there are some aspects meaningful lives share. When I see someone living a meaningful life, their purpose is always centered around leading, caring, protecting, giving, helping, building, educating, healing, or creating.

The power of pursuing a meaningful life goes far beyond what seeking happiness can do for your levels of contentment. We cannot always choose happiness. Sometimes, like Frankl's experience in the death camp, life brings such suffering that the pursuit of happiness is unavailable. But the pursuit of meaning is always available, no matter what.

Frankl wrote, "Ultimately, man should not ask what the meaning of his life is, but rather must recognize that it is he who is asked. In a word, each man is questioned by life; and he can only answer to life by answering for his own life; to life he can only respond by being responsible." About happiness, he wrote, "Happiness cannot be pursued; it must ensue." His experiences and studies led him to the conclusion that happiness only results as a byproduct of pursuing meaning, not as a result of happiness being a person's only goal.

Defining Your Purpose

I don't think one's purpose is so much found as defined.

To tell someone to "find your purpose" makes it seem like life is a treasure hunt, and if you haven't found your purpose yet, you're unlucky or not patient enough.

That being said, I was influenced to open up my perspective on this when I heard Lewis Pugh interviewed on the podcast *Champion's Mojo*.[40] To paraphrase, he says that you must keep drilling for your purpose until you find it. It is like gold; some people find it easily when panning in a stream and others have to drill and drill and then follow the vein they reach. It is indeed a treasure, and yet we all have it.

Our purpose can be an ever evolving and even changing thing. It comes into focus more clearly as we take steps toward what we imagine it to be.

How do you define your purpose today?

It helps to have a standard against which you can measure all opportunities in your life, including opportunities to spend your money when shopping, and experiential opportunities too.

What guides you? Why do you do what you do? Who and what do you love?

We are free to write our own life stories.

But an outline or map helps. Some guiding principles help. Knowing yourself helps.

Questions to Answer

Here are some questions to ask yourself. Think through or write your answers in a journal to help you define your own purpose.

---

40 Episode 37 https://championsmojo.com/episodes

- What three experiences have most impacted the person I am today?
- What is most valuable in my life?
- What are my top three favorite emotions?
- What experiences give me the feelings I want to feel?
- What has been the biggest misfortune in my life so far and how did I deal with it?
- What are three recurring themes in my life so far?
- Who do I look up to and why?
- How can I help other people deal with what has been difficult for me?
- What am I willing to work hard for?
- What makes me feel proud of myself or my actions?
- What will I be most glad about when looking back on my life at the end of it?

Go with your gut on these. You don't have to overthink your answers. They don't ever need to be finalized or shared with anyone else. They can change throughout your life but the themes of what you most value will probably stay more or less the same.

I used to feel panicked that I didn't know my life's purpose or what I would "be when I grew up" but then I realized all I have to do is the next right thing.

If I'm not sure what to do next, then the next right step is to experiment until I find what feels right. Some of my favorite feelings are openness, curiosity, and hope, so this fits in with the kind of learning experiences I love to have. Life is about learning; I believe my gut will guide me.

In my book *Minimalist Living: Decluttering for Joy, Health, and Creativity*, I write about the Minimalist Mission Statement. It's exactly what it sounds like: a 1-3 sentence statement that defines your vision for your home and life. It's a powerful tool to help you zero in on what you want your home and life to look like and feel like.

In this book, I want to help you *free yourself to pursue experiences that fulfill your guiding purpose*. Home in on those experiences that have given you a taste or vision that feels truest to you and closest to your purpose.

I recommend you define your essential purpose in 1-3 sentences. Again, this can change, and you don't have to share it with another soul.

If you're not a fan of journaling, or you just don't feel like putting down this book to take a journaling break, simply take a moment to think about how you would define your purpose today in 1-3 sentences.

Let this purpose guide you to more meaningful experiences and less distracting clutter.

Chapter Four

Freedom

When my husband's job first took us to the Middle East, we lived in the West Bank, very close to the border between Israel and Palestine. Although I was living close to one of the longest ongoing conflicts in the world, it seemed that there wasn't much I could do to help the people on either side.

So, I tried to help a few dogs.

Israel has a culture of rescuing dogs and training them as pets. Palestine, less so. Although a few Palestinians keep pet dogs, most canines born in the wild there are often either put to work as sheep dogs or, sadly, become mistreated street dogs. They may even be poisoned if they are seen as a danger to humans.

One day the most adorable puppy locked eyes with me. She was hanging out by the road next to my home. No collar. Very new to the world, but old enough that she'd grown a soft, plush crop of fur. She was irresistibly cuddly. I lived at the top of a large valley used as grazing ground by local shepherds. I surmised that she was the pup of a sheep dog and she'd wandered away from her mother, whom I couldn't find.

I'd learned that there was a no-kill dog shelter just over the border, in Israel, but to get her there I had to walk through an imposing military checkpoint. There were no humane shelters in Palestine, so this was my only option to help her. Once she got her Israeli pet passport, she'd be able to travel internationally, including back and forth between Israel and Palestine if need be.

I put her in a box on my lap and caught a ride to Qalandia checkpoint. I stood in line to walk across the border. When it was my turn to face the Israeli soldiers and show my passport, I saw that they appeared to be two teenagers, a young man and a young woman. Yes, they were intimidating, fitted as they were with body armor and big guns. But their faces looked so young, and their expressions were open.

Their job was to ensure security at the border and make sure no rules were broken. They peered into the box and told me that no live animals were allowed to cross the border. I explained that the puppy needed help that could only be provided across the border. They shook their heads, apologetic, but firm.

I needed a new strategy. I pulled the puppy from her box and held her up to the bullet-proof glass between me and the soldiers. I let those heavily armed teenagers take a good, long look into those sweet puppy eyes. The seconds seemed to stretch out as both teenagers peered at the canine cuddle bomb. The female soldier looked at me, shook her head and then conferred for a long time with the other soldier.

I shot an apologetic look to the long line of people behind me, waiting in single file to cross the border.

Finally the soldier came out from behind the glass. "*You* cannot *bring* the dog across the border," she said. "But if a dog were to walk across a border by itself, who would stop it?"

She gestured to an invisible line on the floor of the checkpoint building. *The Border*. I set the puppy down, stepped over the line, and then turned back to see if she would follow me into Israel.

The puppy didn't move. "Come on girl," I said, afraid that any moment the soldiers would change their minds about this rather open-hearted interpretation of the rules. But they appeared to be silently cheering for her. Everyone nearby in the checkpoint, Muslim, Jewish, Christian, Whatever, watched as she lifted off her furry little haunches and teetered sideways on her tiny paws. *Come on girl. Cross that border. You need a home,* I thought. I would have adopted her, but I had already rescued one puppy and didn't have room for another. She sniffed the floor, looked up at me, and finally padded across the border and into her new life.

Freedom and Its Many Faces

We all want to be free. Some of us are born on the wrong side of a border. Some of us simply feel trapped by obligations, our financial situation, even our own incessant thoughts. But we all long for the ability to choose our own story.

If you're reading this book, I hope you're living in a country where you have physical freedom and that your civic freedoms are protected. Because addressing those is beyond my scope here.

But I can help you move toward *some* kinds of freedoms. Let's talk about pursuing these: financial freedom, freedom from following the herd, freedom from busyness, and emotional freedom.

Living "Below Your Means"

How do you live free in a world that wants to clutter you up?

"I live free by living below my means but not being critical of those who don't. I try to 'live and let live.' It has brought me peace to not try to 'fix' others who don't want to be fixed."

–June Ann Strickland via the Minimalist Living Facebook page

Sticking to a budget or designing a lifestyle that you know is below your means is wise. If you're spending less than you earn and saving any money at all, you are doing better than 60% of Americans, according to a 2015 financial capability survey.[41] If you're debt-free, you're different from the 77% of Americans who live in debt, according to 2018 research by Northwestern Mutual.[42]

We tend to spend what we make. When we get a raise or make more money, we shift our lifestyle to match our new income level. If we can set our lifestyle level below our means, it can result in a simpler life with more of the experiences we value. This takes effort and focus.

More is not necessarily more. With every financial goal, say, buying a second home or getting a raise or promotion at work, consider the cost, and if you're willing to pay that cost. Will you spend double the time doing boring home-maintenance chores? Will you have to spend more time at work or shift into a role that you don't enjoy as much as your current role? What will you spend the extra money on? Why do you want to achieve the goal?

There's an essay by Derek Sivers about the importance of knowing why you want something before you go after it. He writes, "whatever you choose, brace yourself, because people are always going to tell you that you're wrong. That's why you need to know why you're doing what you're doing. Know

---

[41] http://www.usfinancialcapability.org/downloads/NFCS_2015_Report_Natl_Findings.pdf page 6

[42] https://www.prnewswire.com/news-releases/new-data-personal-debt-on-the-rise-topping-38-000-exclusive-of-mortgages-300696088.html

it in advance. Use it as your compass and optimize your life around it."[43]

Freedom from Convention

In part of her comment earlier in the chapter, June Ann Strickland wrote, "I try to 'live and let live.'"

This attitude of not worrying too much about what other people are doing can free us. Not only because we are free not to try to change or "fix" other people, but because we can *find our own path*. We don't have to follow the herd, nor do we have to recruit a herd of our own to lend credence to what we're doing.

Just because you've found what works for you doesn't mean it will work for everyone. And inversely, just because a certain conventional lifestyle choice seems to work for a lot of people *doesn't mean it will work for you*. And that's okay.

So How do you live free in a world that wants to clutter you up? One way is to stay open to unconventional living. For example, you might rent a home instead of owning one. Home ownership is a conventional goal, a part of the so-called "American Dream," but it comes with a myriad of hidden obligations and expenses. It might not be worth all the work. It's been sold as a worthy goal, as an accomplishment, and a sign of middle-class prosperity but it's not necessarily a choice that brings freedom for everyone. In fact, it tends to tie people down for at least five years, the recommended minimum time to own a home as an investment.

Blogger James Altucher writes about the ills of home ownership. "Every day I see more propaganda about the American Dream of owning the home," he writes in a blog

---

[43] https://sivers.org/why

post entitled "It's Financial Suicide To Own A House."[44] Although I wouldn't put it in such drastic terms, I'm firmly in his camp – at least for now.

As a nomad, I love the ability to rent, and as someone who is not a builder and doesn't enjoy being responsible for the electrical, plumbing, and other systems of a building, I like having the property owner or manager take care of the maintenance and upkeep of the home. It seems odd to expect everyone to know how to maintain or repair all systems in a home, when that is not part of our public education in the USA.

Does the average first-time home buyer know that they'll likely need a plumber, electrician, heating and air specialist, glass installer, painter, pressure washer, and many other professionals if it's an older home? Not to mention how much conscientious professionals cost to hire and how difficult it can be to find them. Also, I've noticed that among home-owning couples, one of the two needs to work from home or work a very flexible job near home in order to make it feasible. This is because home repair and maintenance technicians often give a window of 4-8 hours during which they could possibly show up. Contrast this with my experience as a tenant in an apartment complex employing a full-time property manager. I could give the manager permission to enter the apartment with the necessary professionals and fix the problem when I was not home.

I can see myself owning a home one day. I think having the choice is important. I am not trying to glorify poverty or being forced to rent if you'd like to purchase a home. But right now, I'm not making it an automatic goal in my life just because it's assumed everyone should aspire to it. It seems to me that most people who own a home pour a huge amount of energy, time, and money into managing their property.

---

[44] https://jamesaltucher.com/2015/10/own-house/

Experience Over Stuff

For some, that might be an ideal fit for their interests and a comforting signal of a secure future. For others, the attention and time home ownership requires may be an unwelcome intrusion on something else they'd prefer to be doing.

Creating Less Waste

Living unconventionally can mean making consumer choices that protect our planet from excess waste. This doesn't have to mean living deprived. New and exciting options for living without owning appear all the time. Think your only option is not buying things? Think again. You can rent and borrow to meet your needs and wants, too.

Renting

Companies like Rent the Runway (for designer clothes) make it more fun to rent than to buy. When you buy items, you need to consider the entire life cycle of the item. When you rent items you might normally buy, you get a chance to use something that is new-to-you, but does not come with the hassle of figuring out what to do with it when you no longer want or need it. Rent the Runway and other clothing rental companies will often take care of the dry cleaning for you, so that's another hassle you don't have to worry about.

There are many things you can rent instead of buy. Not just homes and cars, but clothes, handbags, luggage, and jewelry. You can even rent chickens and goats, according to a blog post by Erin Huffstetler entitled "13 Things You Didn't Know You Could Rent."[45]

If you're thinking about getting into a hobby, but want to dip your toe in the water first, there are many hobby-related things you can rent to help you decide. Think skis, kayaks, surf boards, guitars, roller skates, and bowling balls. You're

---

[45] https://www.thebalanceeveryday.com/things-you-did-not-know-you-could-rent-4147332

saving yourself potentially thousands of dollars if you decide the hobby just isn't your thing.

There are many companies that rent hobbyist items, but there are also services that connect regular people who own things to each other so they can participate in the "sharing economy." According to a paper published in the *Journal of the Association for Information Science and Technology*, what the authors term "collaborative consumption," "operates through technological platforms, such as a website or mobile app, yet relies heavily on social dynamics for the actual sharing and collaboration."[46] Airbnb and Uber are well-known innovators and creators of the new sharing economy.

While renting is usually more expensive, over time, than purchasing an item you use long term, if you're a short term, or very occasional user, it might end up saving you money. The biggest benefit of renting is that a given item is actually getting used repeatedly for its intended purpose, not sitting in someone's closet. Renting equals less waste.

Borrowing

It's the free version of renting. Got something in your house you rarely use? Say, a glue gun you only use once a year to make holiday decorations? I bet you'd be happy to lend it to your neighbor. And maybe they'll let you borrow something in return.

Borrowing can be more complicated than it sounds, thus leading many people to give up and just go to the store and buy exactly what they want. Borrowing means knowing your neighbors, being willing to ask for a favor, and that the lender can trust that the borrower will return the item in good condition. I once had a neighbor who was happy to let

---

[46] https://people.uta.fi/~kljuham/2016-hamari_at_al-the_sharing_economy.pdf

me borrow any one of his many tools – if I could find it. Each time I went looking for a specific screwdriver, it was in a different place. It was frustrating to spend so much time looking for what I needed. But, borrowing has advantages like getting to know your neighbors, saving you money, and being eco-friendly. Plus, it feels good when you can help someone out by lending them something they need.

Travel

Travel – or simply having the option to travel – is a great barometer of various types of freedom. Many people dream of traveling or living abroad, but few seem to follow through. This makes a life with lots of travel rather unconventional.

Traveling is a great way to enhance your personal growth. Meeting people who are different than me expands my capacity for empathy and curiosity. We also discover that humans everywhere are very similar. It's a paradox—you get to see great diversity in the way we live, look, sound, eat, and perceive the world– and yet you also see that deep down, we aren't that different. It seems to me that those who travel more seem to have less fear and antipathy towards those who are very different from them.

The ability to pick up and go is another way people measure their freedom, as you'll see in the next chapter.

Time Freedom

How do you live free in a world that wants to clutter you up?
"Refuse to be busy, say no to things, and understand I cannot do everything. Knowing my limits is okay even if people see me as 'lazy' or 'uninvested.' I would rather be seen this way than feel stressed and overwhelmed."

–Alice Sandilands via the Minimalist Living Facebook Page

Expectations that other people place on our lives can seem overwhelming. They can add so much pressure that we say "yes" without even realizing why or how it happened. This happens especially with our schedules. Living free is about ending the glorification of "busy."

Consider the commitments cluttering up your schedule. This is such a sensitive topic. I'm a big fan of *doing what you say you are going to do*. I believe it's really important to have this kind of integrity. However, if you have already over-committed yourself, it's best to confess and withdraw from the event or commitment as soon as you suspect you may have overbooked yourself. That's preferable to dropping out at the last minute or failing to show up without a word of communication.

The pain of disentangling yourself from commitments you never should have said yes to in the first place can be a powerful motivating factor when you feel the discomfort of saying "no" in the future. I remember how disappointed others feel when I have to withdraw from something I've committed to. I use that as a sort of cautionary tale to help me really make sure that I can do something without overextending myself before I say "yes." Over time, this builds trust with the people around you who know you're careful about saying "yes" only when you really mean it.

Trouble Saying No

Saying "no" is hard for us agreeable people-pleasers. If, like me, you have trouble saying "no," try sprucing your "no" up instead of saying it baldly. You can spruce up your "no," by saying something positive before and after, like:

- "I think it's great you're doing that, but I can't attend. I hope you enjoy."

- "Right now, I wish I could say yes, but I can't because of my other commitments. Maybe next time."

Experience Over Stuff

- "I think you're an interesting person, but I don't think we should go on a date. Thank you for asking."
- "Thank you for inviting us, but we have other plans on that day. Looking forward to seeing you next time."

When I am interviewing to hire someone for my business, but that candidate didn't work out, I send an email that reads something like this:

Thank you so much for the time you spent on this. I think I have found another option that works a little better for me at this time. I'm sending you best wishes for another even better opportunity to come your way since this one didn't work out.

Note that usually no further explanation on *why* you're saying no is needed or wanted. I find that a person who asks for a follow-up explanation may be trying to sell me something. For example, I call to cancel some recurring service, and the company's representative says, "Why are you canceling?" In that case, I can say, "no explanation needed."

You can also use the Slow Down Rule. This rule comes in handy for any time in your life you feel uncertainty coupled with a pressure to respond quickly and decisively. There is really only one time you need to respond instantly, and that is when you or a nearby person's life is in imminent danger. Otherwise, you can always say, "Let me think about it," or variations such as "Let me sleep on it," or "That's something for me to consider."

That way you can weigh the event or commitment against your values, your schedule, and your gut feelings.

Space to Breathe or Nap

I find that even if I really want to do something, it's a match for my values, and I have time for it in my schedule, I still should not always say "yes." I don't really thrive in my life unless I also have unbooked time. I thrive on quite a bit of unclaimed time, time during which I have not made plans with anyone.

I think of this free time as "margin," as in, the blank space on either side of words on a page. I learned this from my mom, Maria Parker, a world-record-setting athlete and trailblazing CEO of a bicycle company called Cruzbike. She is also excellent with time management and other topics and you'll see her quoted throughout this book.

The pages of my life need to have wide margins. However, it's hard to explain to someone that I need some time to be busy doing nothing, so I don't usually mention this to people. I simply try not to book more than one main activity for each day.

I use wide margins to do projects with my kids, cuddle with my husband, nap, dream up ideas for books, businesses, and inventions, go out to coffee or lunch, stare off into space, make art, organize my closet, or do nothing but enjoy some solitude. It's not that these things can't be scheduled; of course they can. It's that I really enjoy lots of flexible time to do whatever I want. And over time, I've learned that this isn't something optional that I enjoy once in a while. Huge margins are vital to keeping my happiness levels high and my stress levels low. I have to constantly be on the lookout for the insidious mental chatter that reflects false conventional and cultural beliefs that tell me my value and quality of life come from productivity and *doing* rather than from *being*.

A Life That's True

Bronnie Ware was a palliative care nurse for many years. She brought her excellent listening ability to the job where she was required to sit for hours at the bedsides of the sick and

Experience Over Stuff

dying. She wrote a blog post[47] about what she learned about the regrets of the terminally ill people she cared for. The post went viral.

One of the biggest regrets of dying people, according to Ware, was that they didn't live a life that was true to themselves. Ware wrote that the most common regret she heard among her dying patients was "I wish I'd had the courage to live a life true to myself, not the life others expected of me."

Living a life that is true to yourself – that's freedom in its essence.

But it's not always easy to live authentically.

Like I wrote in Chapter Two, when I was in high school I was very shy and self-conscious. My shyness wasn't a natural expression of being introverted. Rather, it was based on the fear that if I were true to myself, something bad would happen. Maybe people wouldn't like me, or I might say something that hurt someone. I might seem stupid, strange, or dull.

If I lived life out loud, I could fail. I might fall flat on my face. Ouch.

Of course I would. We all fall flat on our faces sometimes. We all make mistakes and we all fail on the way to success.

Two things helped me overcome these worries and blossom into someone who could confidently be herself.

The first thing was that my mom – a natural extrovert – convinced me that my constant self-consciousness was selfish. She said that we are all mostly concerned about our own lives – our feelings, our concerns, our problems, and

---

[47] https://bronnieware.com/blog/regrets-of-the-dying/

our goals. She told me people didn't go around spending all day thinking about me. They had their own issues.

That advice really helped me open up more and be less afraid to embarrass myself. I learned to ask people questions about their life and listen to the answers. I learned that she was right – most people wanted to be heard and to connect. They didn't care that I was shy or nervous.

The other thing that helped me was meeting Rachel, who became my best friend in high school. She was also a new kid at the school, having moved to the area after I did, but she had a social grace that I lacked. She made friends easily and within a few months she had become one of the most popular students at school. I learned a lot from her and she helped me come out of my shell in a way that I will always be grateful for.

After high school, I went forth in life determined to be true to myself and to not keep my words and feelings locked inside like I used to. I would go up to strangers at parties and talk to them even if I was nervous. I would volunteer to be the first to share in a group setting. I would raise my hand and offer opinions and questions in my college classes. I would study abroad and meet new people in new languages.

It wasn't always easy to open up and be myself, although it became easier and easier over the years. The reward has been a fulfilling life of deep and enriching friendships and shared adventures.

Emotional Freedom
The final sort of freedom I want to address is emotional freedom, which for me is inextricably linked to spirituality. We'll talk more about spirituality in Chapter Ten, but for now I want to say that for me, spirituality is feeling connected to all that is, was, and ever shall be.

For me, this connectedness feels peaceful, unbound, ecstatic, blissful, held, loving, and wondrous.

Painful emotions get in the way of my highest spiritual expression. But, as they say, the obstacle is the path. The pain is the way to my deepest spiritual expression.

Emotions can't be controlled, but they can be accepted. Emotions come from thoughts. Our thoughts are an ongoing broadcast that can't be controlled, but they can be framed. In other words, our thoughts *about* our thoughts really matter.

Framing Your Thoughts

Eckhart Tolle writes:

"The beginning of freedom is the realization that you are not "the thinker." The moment you start watching the thinker, a higher level of consciousness becomes activated. You then begin to realize that there is a vast realm of intelligence beyond thought, that thought is only a tiny aspect of that intelligence. You also realize that all the things that truly matter – beauty, love, creativity, joy, inner peace – arise from beyond the mind. You begin to awaken."

—From Practicing the Power of Now: Essential Teachings, Meditations, and Exercises from the Power of Now. [48]

Tolle's book *The Power of Now* was one of those life-changing reads for me. I read about thirty or forty books each year, and I would list *The Power of Now* among my top-ten most life-changing ever, especially for people who spend a lot of time feeling stuck in negative thinking cycles.

Another book that is completely different in tone, but on a similar topic is *You Can be Happy No Matter What* by

---

[48] https://www.goodreads.com/work/quotes/3437032-practicing-the-power-of-now-essential-teachings-meditations-and-exerc

Richard Carlson. Part of happiness – certainly not all, but part – is permission. We choose happiness and give ourselves permission to do so even when things aren't going well.

It's okay to be happy even if something terrible has happened. But the heart of the book's message is that we can't exactly control every one of our thoughts. That gave me a lot of relief because I'd somehow gotten the message that I could and should be a positive thinker. I shouldn't allow negative thoughts in my mind at all. But I could never do this. Worried thoughts appear in a flash and there's not much I can do about them. Carlson's message is that we can choose *not to take our own thoughts as seriously*. This is what I mean by framing our thoughts.

Carlson says that many people have a thought, and then spend a lot of time worried about what it means that they had the thought. Whereas when someone else has the same thought, they could be okay with writing it off. *It was just a thought.*

Being mindful of our thoughts, observing them while not necessarily taking them all seriously, is a step forward on the path to emotional freedom.

Chapter Five

Creating Your Experiences

I was on a playground in Kyiv, Ukraine with my preschool-age son. He enjoyed the sandbox while I chatted with another mom. She was American, and was introducing me to a Ukrainian nanny, whom we'll call Lena.

I said hi and started speaking to Lena. But her expression soon revealed that she didn't understand my rapid-fire English.

"Ah," I said. "I know a little Russian." I thought this would be a great time to practice the tiny amount of Russian I'd been learning. Lena looked at me hopefully. A small crowd had gathered. They looked at me too. I searched my mind and came up with a phrase that I thought meant, "I eat sushi."

What I said was, "Я ест суши."

Lena's face showed confusion. "That's not correct," she said.

I felt a rush of embarrassment.

My first time trying out a full sentence of Russian in public, and I had boldly proclaimed, "I am sushi."

Not an auspicious beginning.

But then again, I was a beginner. Beginnings don't have to forecast future greatness. They just have to be a start.

Travel often brings experiences of ignorance and failure like my playground language learning. Any stretching experience does. Anytime we start something new, go somewhere new, or try to grow in any particular area of our lives, we're going to stumble through it.

The outer reaches of our comfort zones are full of obstacles that can trip us up.

But what some people call tripping, others call dancing. It's all in how you look at it. What most people who seek adventure want is to walk that line between tripping and dancing. It's an experience.

Taking responsibility for an experience over stuff lifestyle means changing your focus. It means putting yourself in situations where you get to dance – even if it means you stumble a few times while learning to tango.

Living the experience over stuff life means asking yourself what experience you desire. We often ask ourselves "what do I want?" and what we are really thinking is "what *experience* do I want?

In an article called "5 Reliable Findings from Happiness Research,"[49] John M. Grohol, founder and editor-in-chief of Psych Central, writes, "Focus on experiences, not stuff. People who spend their time and money on doing things together — whether it be taking a vacation to someplace other than home or going on an all-day outing to the local zoo — report higher levels of happiness than those who buy a bigger house, a more expensive car, or more stuff."

---

[49] https://psychcentral.com/blog/5-reliable-findings-from-happiness-research/

How do you live free in a world that wants to clutter you up?

"I try to enjoy experiences, not stuff. My memories of living in the moment are reward enough."

–Kelley Allison via the Minimalist Living Facebook page

Living in the moment. It sounds important. But what does it really do for you? It elevates your experience.

Anne Lamott wrote a book called *Help, Thanks, Wow: The Three Essential Prayers.* It is about exactly what you'd think – how "help," "thanks," and "wow," are the three essential prayers. It is written, of course, with the particular beauty and pathos only Anne Lamott can bring. Choosing experience over stuff turns more of our everyday moments into the last prayer, that "wow," prayer. It's an expression of wonder. Amazement. Awe.

Experience over stuff living is not so much about seeking peak experiences as it is about noticing *the peak you're on right now.* It's not about getting to the top of the mountain; it's about noticing you're on a mountain in the first place. And when you get to the top, it's about savoring that fully before moving on to plan the next hiking trip.

Creating your experience is both about curating your experiences (planning a hiking trip and taking it) and being fully present (enjoying the hike you're on).

It's easy to spend all day responding to the pings and dings of our device-driven lives. We can even seek out these sorts of shallow distractions to allay boredom or sweep away unwanted emotions. Instead, let's curate deeper and more meaningful pleasures.

Let's call partially distracted checking of social media a "mid-level" experience. Our goal here is to be greedier for a higher level of experience. Let's level up through presence.

There's nothing wrong with checking email or social media or occasionally having diffuse focus when we are tired or stressed. But a full day of that won't feel like a rich experience. It's also unlikely to be productive or meaningful.

Travel

For many, including me, travel is a peak experience. For me, it's the full package: it's challenging but also filled with excitement, fun, and relaxation. If you want to travel, but for some reason find it difficult to actually make it happen, whether because of fears or financial concerns, you're not alone. Generalized anxiety about going to a new place is something to talk through with a friend or therapist. Don't let it hold you back from doing something you really want to do. You may also be concerned about your responsibilities at home. The best thing to do is save up and buy a nonrefundable plane ticket well in advance. That means you're committed, but it also gives you time to plan for your responsibilities to be covered while you are gone.

Showing Off Vs. Living

A 2016 article on CNBC says, "Millennials are prioritizing their cars and homes less and less, and assigning greater importance to personal experiences — and showing off pictures of them."[50]

The article's subtext was that millennials are focusing more on experiences as a way to avoid "fear of missing out," or as a way to brag that they are part of an experience that is exclusive or superior. Whether or not that is true, it's helpful to ask ourselves why we want to share photos and videos of our experiences. Let's share out of a desire to connect, not to make others feel inferior.

---

[50] https://www.cnbc.com/2016/05/05/millennials-are-prioritizing-experiences-over-stuff.html

Whatever generation we are part of, let's care more about experiences, connection, and sharing than we do about amassing a collection to show our worth. Let's find our value in who we are inherently. Let's know who we are and share our truth – in person and on social media because those are the platforms where we are having important conversations, connecting, and sharing our lives.

Like I wrote earlier, it's not only millennials who are decluttering and embracing simplicity – it's people of retirement age and beyond, too. A recent book in the genre of home organizing and decluttering is called *The Gentle Art of Swedish Death Cleaning: How to Free Yourself and Your Family from a Lifetime of Clutter.* My neighbor, who is getting older, told me she'd been spending her time in the spring 2020 quarantine due to the Corona Virus by going through drawers. "Going through drawers?" I wanted her to elaborate. "Yes," she said. "I have so many papers. There's no one else to do it after I go."

It's not only the consideration of one's eventual passing that motivates a newfound minimalism. Swaths of the boomer generation are reaching retirement age and taking to the road. These folks are bringing lots of energy and a sense of adventure to what they plan on being a long retirement filled with fun and exploration. Michael Gallant commented in the Minimalist Living Facebook Community, writing, "You could probably classify RVers as a distinct subculture of minimalists. We prefer experiences over things. Downsizing to 300 s.f. motorhome from a 2000+ s.f. house is an exacting exercise in what is needed."

Although many RVers are retirees, some of them are working in the new economy as digital nomads. Others are bringing their homes with them for seasonal work. Some are going where they want to go and following the work or finding work where they are, like couple Tommy and MacKenzie, who live in a van, and shared about life with blogger Wes

Siler.[51] "It takes a lot of humility to make this work, but we both see a lot of value in doing it this way," said MacKenzie.

I think humility is a recurring trend when embracing simple, experiential living. One has to be humble because life will not always look like the cultural expectations of "success" if you are being yourself and living the life you want to live.

Love Over Stuff

One big concern when people read one of my blogs or books is what their spouse or partner or roommate will think about minimalism.

Sometimes one partner's minimalism can clash with the other partner's tendency to collect things. One of the most common concerns people bring up in the Minimalist Living community on Facebook is that their spouse or partner doesn't seem to agree with their own attitude toward stuff. It's pretty common that we marry someone who is our opposite in this area.

In my own marriage, although my husband and I are both minimalists who emphasize experiences over ownership, we both express it so differently that it sometimes causes conflict. The things we choose to keep and the time we choose to spend maintaining, organizing, and shopping varies. We don't always agree, and we are *both* enthusiasts of simple living, so imagine the strife that can crop up when one partner is a minimalist and the other is a collector.

The answer is to not try to change your partner. Apply minimalism in your life, in the domains that are yours. For example, your closet, your clothes, and any area of your life that won't affect or bother your partner.

---

[51] https://www.outsideonline.com/2170691/how-live-vanlife-without-it-sucking

Your partner may be influenced by the benefits minimalism brings to your life, or they may not. Just enjoy minimalism for yourself.

Relationships Over Stuff

Claire Ord emailed me to tell me about a time she chose experience over stuff. She wrote, "Looking around my 8-year-old daughter's room racking my brain thinking of gift ideas for Xmas, but can't think of anything. She already has every toy and they sit in the toy box, untouched. I've decided this year instead of toys, I'm making her a box with 6 envelopes inside. One envelope for each week of the school holidays to open at the beginning of each week. Inside there will be a different prepaid activity to do – movie tickets, bowling voucher, paddle boarding voucher. It will be a gift that keeps on giving every week; I can't wait."

Spending time with people we love is a great way to choose experience over stuff.

Creativity Over Drama

We create our experiences, whether we do so consciously or unconsciously. Do you know anyone who seems to create or attract a lot of unnecessary drama in their relationships? Is that person you? It happens to the best of us. I've noticed people like this are often highly creative. However, their creativity isn't being applied to their life in a constructive way. Instead, it gets destructive. If we don't have a creative outlet in our lives, something challenging to make or build towards, we can become mean and cruel.

People repeat unhealthy patterns in their relationships because they aren't creating something meaningful. Once there's a sense of purpose, we see unhealthy patterns drop away. They were just distractions between meaningful, creative projects.

How do you get creative? Start with a good question. It can be a small question, like, "How can I make my shoulders stronger?" or "How can I make this square of fabric into something useful?" Or it can be a bigger question, like "How can I make giving birth a more empowering experience for more women?" Not coincidentally, that last question is one my sister and I are trying to answer at BirthPractice.com.

Keep a notebook of *your* questions and answers. Once you fill it, go through it, and save any ideas that you're still curious about.

"I question. It's not always a comfortable way to be, but it is vital to making good art. People tend to like certainty, but it's art's ability to transform us and to help us see our world in a new way that interests me. And the only way to shift other people's paradigms is to start by shifting my own."

—Gwenn Seemel, Artist & Free Culture Advocate interviewed for my book *The Wealthy Creative*

Giving: A Good Experience

In their book *Why Good Things Happen to Good People: How to Live a Longer, Healthier, Happier Life by the Simple Act of Giving*, Steven Post and Jill Neimark detail all the ways that giving benefits us. As an experience, giving can be healing. In fact, in one study cited in the book, givers who dedicated themselves to listening compassionately to people with a disease healed faster than the recipients of that listening support. And here's what really awed me: the givers – the listeners in the study– had the same disease as those they were listening to.

People who looked for opportunities to give that used their natural strengths and talents seemed to reap the most benefits from it.

Write the Book, Save the World

There are many different ways to give. I wrote an essay called "Write the Book, Save the World,"[52] about giving through writing for the website *Write to Done*. It's a blog for writers. I'm reprinting an edited and abridged version of the essay below in case giving for you is also writing. But if it's not, feel free to insert whatever sort of giving aligns with your natural skills and talents in place of "writing the book."

***

Two Ways to Save the World

My husband and I both work hard at two very different jobs.

Sometimes I compare my job as a writer and publisher to his and I wonder if I'm bringing enough value to the world and helping enough people.

You see, he works with a large nonprofit organization that helps vulnerable populations. His job is to help refugee families find safe housing and help save children from dangerous situations.

Meanwhile, I'm tooling around on the page, creating a fictional world inhabited by mermaids.

He's saving lives, literally.

I'm saving lives, in literature.

Does this Work Matter?

As a result of comparing my work to his (and let's be honest — as a result of simply being human), I sometimes have doubts about how important it is to finish my current writing project.

---

[52] https://writetodone.com/write-the-book-save-the-world/

I wonder if anyone will care. Or worse, I worry if I'll be criticized for putting this out there.

I know I'm not alone. I ask myself why I'm writing all the time. On good days, I think about my readers and how they've benefited from my writing in the past. But it's hard to keep the people who will potentially benefit from my book (or any writing project) in mind when I'm alone, writing for hours on end.

I have doubts about the value of my continued writing all the time even, though I can head over to Amazon to read dozens of positive reviews of my previous books. The proof that my books connect with readers is right there online. Still, I'm not always a paragon of confidence.

There are more days than I'd like to admit where it can be hard to find the motivation to keep going. I know that for emerging writers, these feelings of uncertainty can be even more crippling since they have very little feedback from their work.

In fact, many writers never even finish one book because they are paralyzed by self-doubt. They are afraid their books won't connect with anyone — not even one person. And this fear is just one of a list of fears, including comparing themselves with other writers and worrying they come up short.

Here's What to Ask Yourself

- What if your work helped just one person?
- What if your work connected with one person and colored their life with joy for one moment?
- What if it gave just one person a powerful connective experience, a sense that they aren't alone?

Would one be enough for you? For many people, it is. If their work connected with or helped just one other person in a meaningful way, they could keep going confidently.

Writing for One Person

What if by finishing your book, you could save the world? If that seems like an unrealistic suggestion, consider your book helping just one person cope, escape, connect, or hope.

In the first season of the 2006 NBC hit series *Heroes*, a mantra is repeated: "Save the cheerleader, save the world."

It tapped into a truth: we help the world by helping one person at a time. We might even save the world by saving one person at a time. As writers, we trade in the currencies of ideas; ideas are powerful when it comes to helping and changing people.

For example, reading books got me through many a difficult, lonely, depressed, or anxious time in my life. Books are friends when the people I love aren't around. I've learned, escaped, laughed, and cried with books. I've bonded with fellow bookworms and learned insights about them in book clubs. Have books saved my life? Maybe.

Nonfiction books have let me know I'm not alone. Fiction books have helped me escape when life gets too heavy. If the authors of those books had decided not to write, if they'd let self-doubt halt them, I wouldn't have benefited from the ideas they shared. I do not doubt that my life would be diminished in many ways if they had listened to doubt.

Envision the one person you are writing for, the one person who will connect deeply with your work. That's all you have to do to maintain the confidence to keep writing.

Even if your book helps or connects with only one person, it's worth it, because one life enhanced can have a positive ripple effect on the world.

Write the book. Save the world. Start today.

***

Core Desired Feelings

Peak Experiences involve flow and using your strengths to do something meaningful. They feel amazing. However, not every moment of our lives is going to be a peak experience. That's okay. But to nudge things in the right direction, it helps to identify how you want to feel.

Through her Desire Map website, motivational author and speaker Danielle LaPorte helps people define their "Core Desired Feelings."[53]

Core Desired Feelings are what they sound like – how you want to feel. You can also think of them as your target emotions. How do you want to feel and what experiences will get you there? What are your favorite emotions and what are you doing, saying, and focusing on when you feel them?

Do you have your answer?

Do more of that.

There are many ways to get to a feeling, and different people will choose different paths.

When we say, "I want to be a millionaire," for example, we mean something about the way we want to feel. Maybe we mean, "I want to feel financially free," or "I want to feel powerful," or "I want to feel important." Financial freedom is a great goal to shoot for, but if we don't identify the underlying feeling, we risk chasing an accomplishment and never enjoying the feeling that we were after in the first place. We risk actually achieving the goal but having it feel empty.

---

[53] https://www.thedesiremap.com/

However, if we are able to identify the target emotion, the way we think the goal will make us feel, like *powerful*, for example, then we can enhance our life by doing the things that we know make us feel powerful along the way to the quantitative goal like how much money we want in our bank account or the number we want to see on the scale.

Maybe we can even accomplish that powerful feeling today, by going to the gym and feeling the power in our bodies as we pump iron, or by blocking negative people on social media and feeling the power we have to shape our people-scape. These tastes of our target emotions can keep us fueled with the intangibles like motivation and willpower and fun along the way to achieving our big, measurable goals.

We are chasing feelings, not goals. Goals can be achieved or not, but they don't always give us the feelings we are after. And if they do, it's for a fleeting moment. Instead, build your life around the way you want to feel. Choose healthy habits that consistently get you feeling the way you want to feel, and then use those positive feelings to keep the cycle of motivation going.

In *The Big Leap*,[54] Gay Hendricks writes that most of us have more trouble feeling good than feeling bad. Good things happen to us and it's hard to let ourselves enjoy those things. We have a setting – like a climate control system set to a certain temperature – of how good we can feel. Our beliefs keep that thermometer setting in one place. But with conscious effort we can move the thermometer setting and allow ourselves to feel better and better.

---

[54] https://www.goodreads.com/work/quotes/6572235-the-big-leap-conquer-your-hidden-fear-and-take-life-to-the-next-level

Alternative Activities

How do you live free in a world that wants to clutter you up?

"Fill your life with alternative activities that are free but fill your soul. Hiking, biking, reading a good book. Visiting friends etc. This change to minimalism has shown me how much more free time I have not going shopping every weekend."

–Cesira Kelleher via the Minimalist Living Facebook page

What are the "alternative activities that fill your soul?"

Mine are:

- Reading
- Writing
- Walking outside
- Looking at the trees and flowers outside my window
- Talking to a dear friend or family member
- Sitting on the floor with my kid building a Lego tower
- A free yoga class in the park
- Organizing my stuff

I'll bet your list is more interesting – to you. That's what's great about being a human. We're all unique. There are lots of experiences that cost money, but there are lots of great "alternative" experiences that are free and worth filling your life with.

Live the Life You Want
How do you live free in a world that wants to clutter you up?

"Be organized, declutter, surround yourself with things and people you love, live life the way you want to create it, not another person's, and budget wisely."

–Reina Hada via the Minimalist Living Facebook page

Function Over Prestige

I'll end this chapter on creating experiences by saying that we do need stuff. I'm not anti-stuff. I don't villainize shopping. There are lots of things that make the experience of life easier, more fun, more convenient, more comfortable, and simply better. I enjoy nice things, things like my peshtemal towel, my camera gear, and my collection of jewelry. There's nothing wrong with being attached to things as long as those attachments don't cost you your joy. If the idea of your stuff burning or being damaged in a flood makes you feel panicked, you might want to take a look at the beliefs behind the panic. Are they true beliefs?

Ultimately, ask yourself what function your things serve. And by the way, having something simply because it's beautiful is enough of a function. We need beauty in our lives. Beware of having things because of prestige, which simply means because of what others think about it. Chasing prestige is a losing battle.

Choose a battle you can win. Choose stuff you love simply because you love it. Choose and create experiences for the same reason.

Chapter Six

Where the Heart Is

My friend shared on Instagram before and after photos of her children's bedrooms that she'd recently redecorated. Prior to the refresh, the rooms were a bit messy; typical children's rooms. Afterwards, as you might suspect, the bedrooms were clean and tidy. The caption read: "Befores and Afters. Now I can relax." There was a bathtub emoji.

There's something so relaxing about being in a tidy space. The cleaning itself isn't relaxing, so what is it about a visually clear space that feels so good to be in? It's the spaciousness, the sense of possibility, and the sense that all is right in our world. If everything is in place, it is proof that we have power in our lives. We are free to do what we want at home.

Experiences of freedom and possibility often start at home. Home is important, not just because it's where the heart is, but also because it's where we start and finish each day. We have the power to simplify our homes. We can make home a place to relax or be productive. In a world filled with chaos beyond control, home is a space to shape and mold as we desire.

Although this book is about your whole life, your home is the locational center. We spend so much of our lives at home. It's important that our homes are thoughtful places that make us feel like the best version of ourselves.

A Smaller Home
How do you live free in a world that wants to clutter you up?

"When I realized our home isn't too small, we just have too much. Material things are not important, the people in your life are. Less is definitely more."

–Julie Knott via the Minimalist Living Facebook Page

Homes don't have to be large to meet our needs and be wonderful places. A small space can be beautiful. In many ways, a smaller home is better. It may allow you to live in a better location. (Less house in a better location may be more affordable than a big house in an area that is not desirable or requires a soul-sucking commute to work). It will cost less to heat, maintain, and you'll spend less time cleaning it or paying to have it cleaned.

When most people think they need more space, they start looking into renting or buying a bigger home, (or a storage unit). What they may actually need is to look around and free up some space they already have and refresh the decor. The benefits of a smaller home will allow a person to move towards an experience over stuff life.

Free Up Space
Make space. Declutter. Become a minimalist.

Check your closets and see if they can be turned into what you need. For example, an office could become an office or a nursery. Many large closets aren't necessary for storage if you're a minimalist and can be turned into valuable private space.

In a prior apartment I lived in, I turned a small sliding-door closet into a writing office. I loved it. I hung a tiny crystal lamp from the clothing rod above my head; it lit the space beautifully. I put my favorite large piece of wall art right next to me so it entirely covered the ugly inner wall of the closet. I wrote a lot in that closet.

I've also heard of people recording podcasts in closets. I can imagine a small closet could be easily padded to make a nice audio recording studio.

Double duty storage furniture can also solve space problems. For inspiration, look to the tiny house movement, or solutions used in RVs and boats. Consider storage benches, futons, Murphy beds, and fold-down tables.

How to Declutter

If you're not quite a minimalist, but want to be, I'll list a few things you can do here that will help. For more information, read my book *Minimalist Living: Decluttering for Joy, Health, and Creativity*.[55]

There are two main ways you can tackle clutter in an entire home. You can go room by room, or category by category. Room by room would be, for example, starting with your bedroom, then moving to the hallway, then the kitchen. Category by category means listing out your things in categories, for example, "books," and "toiletry items." Each person's list will be a little different. You want categories of manageable sizes that you can tackle in time-chunks that make sense to you and don't seem overwhelming. For some, this will be 15-minutes a day until the job is finished. Others will want to do three 10-hour chunks over a 3-day weekend.

For each space or category, you can choose to "gaze" or "blaze." Gazing is what I call the more traditional route, and it means you examine each item individually, asking your own set of filter questions, such as "do I need it?," "Do I love it?" and the like, before deciding to get rid of it or keep it.

---

[55] https://www.amazon.com/Minimalist-Living-Decluttering-Health-Creativity-ebook/dp/B00H9J8C64

Blazing is my own super-fast method. It requires courage but is the fastest way to declutter. I don't recommend it for spaces or categories that include important paperwork or family heirlooms, but for everything else, it can work well. To blaze, you pull everything out of a given space without examining each individual item. You place all the items in your discard box or bag. Then, without consulting the discard pile, you consider the now-empty space. What do you actually need in there? What do you actually want in there? Put only those things back. Everything else goes in the discard pile.

To make blazing easier, you can hold your discards, labeled as such, for a period of 60-90 days or as long as you need. Put the box away on a high shelf or in a little-used area of your home such as a basement or attic. After that time, if you haven't missed anything out of the box, you can feel secure in letting it leave your life for good.

Maintenance

How do you live free in a world that wants to clutter you up?

"If something new comes in, something old gets donated. For example, if I buy a new shirt, I donate one that I have. That keeps the clutter way down and helps someone else."

–Sherry Schnebly via the Minimalist Living Facebook page

A "One in one out" policy is easy and fun to say, but it's hard to maintain. I'll be honest – I am not able to keep this as a functioning policy in my home. And it's not only because of my husband and children – it's me too. I definitely don't get rid of an item for every item I bring into the house each time. What works better for me is to do seasonal clean-outs, which I'll talk about later.

However, if "one in one out" is something that is motivating and doable for you, I say go for it.

One kind of ongoing maintenance I can handle is an ongoing giveaway pile. That, combined with being honest with myself about whether I'll ever wear something again – is my secret to a minimal wardrobe.

For example, if I notice a hole in the seam of my shirt, I'll assess how easy and quick it will be to fix. Sure, I have a sewing kit and can easily fix the hole. But will I? I fix the garment immediately if I have time. Otherwise I put it to the side. If I haven't fixed it after a couple of weeks, it's probably never going to get fixed and it goes into the giveaway or recycle pile.

Regarding non-clothing items, I regularly throw things into the giveaway pile. I hold the pile for a while so I don't accidentally get rid of something I wanted to keep. It's a lot easier to pull something out of the giveaway pile than it is to juggle clutter, so I err on the side of throwing things in my giveaway pile, even if I'm not sure I want to give it away. The pile becomes a staging area. If I haven't pulled anything out of the pile in 6-12 weeks, I know that I'm not going to miss anything in it. Even if I do miss something, which happens occasionally, I'm going to be okay.

I also use *cyclical living* to keep my home and life simplified. I enjoy tapping into the natural cycles that guide my energy on an annual basis: the four seasons.

Cyclical Simplifying

Minimalist living requires maintenance, but constant, unvaried maintenance begets boredom.

Keep things interesting by following the seasons.

I learned to live in tune with natural cycles and seasons from Kate Northrup, author of *Do Less: A Revolutionary Approach to Time and Energy Management for Ambitious Women*, and Mireille Guiliano, who wrote *French Women for All Seasons*.

Experience Over Stuff

For each season there's a natural way to declutter. Each season will have unique associations for you. Here is how the energy of each season guides my decluttering.

Winter

In the winter, the instinct is to withdraw and create a cozy environment for yourself and your loved ones. It's a time to go within and rest after a busy year. It's a time to celebrate and express gratitude to the people in our lives. We celebrate with feasting, we give gifts, we sing carols. We gaze into the fire and engage in traditions that come along every year and remind us of our past. We also envision our hopes for the future. In the northern hemisphere, when the new year comes around, we set intentions and make plans for what we want to experience the next year.

In winter, the experience over stuff life emphasizes celebrating, giving, resting, and planning.

First, if we are living a simple life or starting to simplify a bit more, we connect with and celebrate the essentials that bring us joy. We do this by remembering what is most important to us and focusing with intention. That means telling the people in our life what they mean to us and celebrating the holidays with a sense of love, connection, and freedom.

 Instead of stressing out about checking all the holiday-tradition boxes, give yourself permission to do only one. Let the rest go. Don't create more work for yourself in an effort to be more festive. My mom remembers that her sister Jenny used to help her with this, saying "You don't have to do it all, Maria, just a wreath on the door is enough." My mom used to stress herself out around the holidays trying to do everything possible to make it magical for us kids. Now she embraces doing less and simplifying her holiday to-do list to the point that she jokingly calls herself the Grinch. Guess what? Holidays at her house are still magical. Dahoo Dores.

What's most important to you in your winter celebrations? Is it to create a cozy atmosphere with candles, cookies, and carols? Is it to take a vacation or spend the holiday somewhere warm and tropical? Do that. But don't take on all the traditions. Traditions are great to the extent they make us feel connected. But as soon as something seems stressful, drop it. You can't rest and go within if you're stressed.

In the winter, we give. It's a time of traditional gift-giving, and also a time of charitable giving. What a wonderful time to clear out the clutter and take your no-longer-wanted clothes, shoes, toys, and household items to an organization that welcomes such donations.

If you have kids, before the holidays is a great time to talk to them about all they have to be grateful for, and to encourage them to give away things they no longer need or want.

Winter is also a great time to make plans for the coming year. It's a time of introspection, and as such is a great time to analyze what went well over the past year – what was essential to your joy and peace, and what didn't go so well. Looking back is something that is easier for some people than for others. I have a hard time with it, personally. I'm very forward-looking. I feel hopeful and excited when I look to the future. Looking to the past sometimes makes me feel heavy. However, I always benefit when I look back and ask myself, "what could I have done better?" or "what can I learn from?" Phrasing the questions that analyze the past in a few different ways can be very helpful. Here are some more helpful questions:

- What was the biggest learning experience of the past year?

- What are three things I'd do differently if I went through that experience again?"

- What are three things I'm glad I handled in the way that I did?

- What advice was I grateful to get this past year?

Analyzing the past is not something to make you feel ashamed or discouraged. It's to make you feel like a whole person, someone able to learn from your experiences as you plan for the future.

Doing an annual review helps you plan for a better year. When it comes to simplifying, you can plan what you are going to declutter, what you're going to drop, and what you're going to keep. What new things will you try? How will you help yourself to live free and breathe easy in the coming year? Will you set a goal or resolution to choose experiences over stuff in the new year?

Spring

Spring is a time of new growth. It's a fertile time when the earth blossoms. This corresponds with implementation time in the plan you made over the winter to simplify your life. It's time to act. By the way, you can start simplifying in any season. But spring is an especially great time to start.

So what does this look like as you emphasize experience over stuff? Well, now's the time to plant seeds for great experiences. It's time to grow the life you want.

Think of the phrase "spring cleaning." We've been cooped up all winter, and now we want some fresh air. We open the windows. We deep clean the house (or hire a cleaning service to do it for us).

It's a chance to declutter anything that is getting in the way of the fresh life we want to live. In the winter, there was an energy of gifting, but in the spring, the energy is more of a weeding energy. A gardener wants to pinch away the weeds in the spring so desired plants can come up.

In the same way, you'll notice in the spring it's easy to acquire by accident or to over-shop. There can be a sort of manic energy. Our optimism can mean our eyes are bigger than our schedules. So, at the same time as you enjoy the new energy spring brings, remember that spring will also bring a crop of weeds. And hey, one person's weeds are another person's treasure. It's not necessarily bad that they are coming up – it's a time to be grateful for all opportunities. Just remember that you can't do everything. In spring you'll get a lot of opportunities and your job is to use your intuition and say yes to the opportunities that feel right – that correspond to your values. Make sure you plant crops you'll be happy to harvest come fall.

Once you've removed clutter, fall in love with your place all over again by refreshing the decor. A fresh coat of paint, different colors, some spruced up thrift store furniture – this doesn't have to be expensive. Paint is the most affordable way to change the look of a room, but some property owners don't let you paint if you're a renter. You can probably talk them into putting a fresh coat of paint in white or a neutral color palette, especially if the wall needs fresh paint anyway.

But if you don't want to paint, try temporary wallpaper[56] or a wall tapestry designed by an independent artist.[57]

Summer

Summer, like winter, is a time to celebrate. But summer has a more outgoing and active energy to it. If spring is about saying yes to certain opportunities, and no to others, summer is about proving your commitment to the opportunities you said yes to and celebrating where you are.

It's a great time to focus on reveling in the freedom that you've created for yourself, whatever that means. It's also a

---

[56] https://www.apartmenttherapy.com/where-to-buy-temporary-and-removable-wallpaper-237551

[57] https://www.redbubble.com/shop/tapestry

time to be more visible, to inspire and help others. It's a great time to partner and connect with the right people who will help you in your experience over stuff journey. What else is it time to do in the summer? It's time to live! This is when your emphasis on experience over stuff really pays off. Will you take that trip you've been saving up for? Will you declare your love to the person you've started that relationship with? Summer is a time to put yourself out there.

If you're starting your journey to a simpler life this summer, then a great place to start is to simply emphasize experiences. Summer is a really creative time so express yourself and live experiences you want to have. Make the plans come true. Don't worry so much about decluttering in the summer; rather, focus on fulfilling experiences.

Autumn

Autumn can be a very busy time, but it's also a time of more structure, more predictability and routine, which can actually have the effect of allowing us to feel less busy or for life to feel less chaotic as we feel a greater sense of control over our lives. This is often when school starts back up and, even if you aren't in school and don't have kids in school, culturally we often sense a "back to school" energy that makes it an efficient, more structured season than summer. There's also an energy of harvest. Harvest energy is a time to get organized. A time to collect and count what you're reaping. We can declutter, yes, but we also tend to want to organize what we have.

There's a "nesting" energy and we want "everything in its place and a place for everything." This is the time when we want to find the perfect container for every closet and shelf and the perfect system. There is not one perfect organization system for your stuff. You can find what works for you. I like to stay inspired by watching YouTube videos that share visually inspiring ways to get organized. This keeps me feeling like organizing is a fun, creative activity.

Fall is a time to edit out anything that isn't working or that is making us feel overwhelmed. Although, instead of editing, you may want to think more in terms of "wrapping up." Are there any big projects or commitments you can wrap up and finish? There's a certain momentum to fall as people tend to want projects to wrap up before the holidays. You can tap into that and get great results. Deadlines can be effective in fall. It's a time of clear delineations. There will be a moment when the last leaf falls from the tree. And then the tree rests.

Fall can be a really busy time – perhaps the busiest season of them all – so make sure you're working on things that are truly meaningful for you. Things that match your essential purpose (see Chapter Three). Otherwise, fall will feel like an overload of stress. Burnout and illness may follow, as you stretch your body to fulfil obligations that aren't matters of the heart for you.

Cycles in Brief

So, when it comes to creating a simple life, the energy of winter is gifting – declutter stuff and give it away. It's also important to rest and go within. In spring, we clean. We dust, scrub, and get to things that don't often get cleaned deeply. In summer, the energy is to move activities outside, to connect, and to focus on creating experiences instead of collecting stuff. In autumn, the energy is to get organized and wrap up projects.

Fear of Missing Out

I asked Simple Living Toolkit community member Claire Ord what gets in the way of choosing experience over stuff. She responded, "F.O.M.O. – fear of missing out. Seeing all the Instagram and Facebook posts of my friends and celebrities having the latest fashions, toys, and homewares makes me envious of that. I feel I need to buy them to keep up with the Joneses, or more like the Kardashians, these days. Their life on screen looks amazing and happy all the time so it makes me think I need those things to be happy too, which never works."

What an honest appraisal of something we all experience. Whether you're watching *Keeping Up with the Kardashians* or just watching anyone enjoy interacting with a consumer product, it's easy to think that the product creates happiness. But happiness is an inside job. This is a message we don't hear enough because it's not a message that sells products.

There's also the phenomenon of curation. Reality TV and social media are carefully edited presentations of someone's life – usually only the best slices. They don't reflect reality – just what a person wants to show as their reality. We can never really know what's going on in someone's life or in a family or a relationship.

Tiny homes, RV life, Van Life, Backpack Life

I can't end this chapter about decluttering at home without addressing the phenomenon of tiny living. Here's what's delightful to me about tiny home living: the fantasy of a home so well-designed, it gives me all the space I need even in half the square footage of what would already be considered a small home.

I'm not sure I would ever actually live in a tiny home. It's hard to imagine my family of four being comfortable in one. However, I know it's possible. I know some tiny homes can accommodate parents and children. For me, tiny homes are mostly about enjoying the idea of something well designed and seeing all the ingenious ways people customize their homes to suit their unique desires.

RV dwellers and van dwellers, like Michael Gallant commented, are a distinct subculture of minimalists. They were minimalists before it was trending and have been coming up with creative ways to live with less stuff for as long as RVs and vans have existed. RV and van living may be the original "experience over stuff" lifestyle as homes that travel with you can allow you to go to the experience or change scenery as often as you'd like.

Another subculture of experience over stuff enthusiasts is backpackers. These folks pack their life up into what can fit into a rucksack and travel the world. Sometimes they go for a few weeks or months, and other times it's a long term lifestyle. In this case, they may call themselves "nomads."

My family and I often call ourselves nomads. While we don't fit our belongings into one backpack each, we do move and travel with a few suitcases each instead of a moving truck or shipping container like most of the other families we meet who have recently moved. We move every couple of months or years. We've lived (for a month or more) in nine cities in four countries over the last five years. Our collective short-term travels in that same time frame add an additional twelve cities and five countries. Owning much less stuff than a typical American family helps us create this experience-rich lifestyle. See where we are today @Genevievewrites on Instagram.

Chapter Seven

Building Your Anti-Impulse-Purchase Armor

I used to love shopping. I remember one Saturday during my college years, I went to the mall with my roommate. After what felt like a few hours of shopping, her energy seemed to be waning. I looked at my watch. We'd be shopping for *nine* hours. To me, the time had flown by. I could shop like it was my job.

Now, I dislike spending a lot of time in shopping malls. I still like shopping online, but now when I am in a large store for more than ten minutes, my feet feel heavy and my eyes get tired of the fluorescent lights and the barrage of marketing images. I'd rather spend time in nature than at the mall. I think this shift happened because I noticed how much better I could feel after a day of activity that was not centered on acquisition. Not only did I feel better, but my credit card bills looked better. Shopping used to be a recreational activity. The excitement of the array of purchasing choices available, the fun of closing in on the next new thing that was going to enhance my life. The well-designed displays were a beautiful aesthetic experience, and the social aspect – shopping together – could bring me closer to friends.

Now I get those thrills – excitement, choices, fun, beauty, and community – for free or cheap through an array of consciously chosen experiences. Instead of being centered around acquisition, the experiences I choose are often centered around nature, exercise, learning, food, spiritual practice, and exploring new places.

And yet, the draw toward shopping is always there. That's because a) we need things and b) there's a lot of money to be made by getting people to buy stuff they need *and* stuff they don't need.

Armor Up

When Tim Ferris asked Derek Sivers what he would put on a billboard, he responded: "I would make a billboard that says 'It Won't Make You Happy,' and I would place it outside any big shopping mall or car dealer. You know what would be a fun project, actually? To buy and train thousands of parrots to say, 'It won't make you happy!' and then let them loose in the shopping malls and superstores around the world. That's my life mission. Anybody in? Anybody with me? Let's do it." (From the book *Tools of Titans* by Tim Ferriss.)

Because of the many subtle and overt marketing messages most of us have to absorb every day, choosing experience over stuff requires protective measures. It's unlikely the billboard or the parrot plan of Derek Siver's imagination will ever be put in place. So let's create our own internal protections against impulse shopping. Let's call these protective measures armor.

As I've written before, experience over stuff isn't about quitting all shopping. Instead, it's about buying less, consciously.

Sounds great, right? In practice, it *is* great. But it requires swimming against the tide. A big obstacle between a cluttered life and a more free and purposeful life is impulse shopping. When we make impulse purchases, we're not intentionally choosing experience over stuff.

There are three main ways to rebel against the clutter marketing machine and the resulting impulse purchases: filter questions, lists and limits.

Pre-purchase Filter Questions

How do you live free in a world that wants to clutter you up?

"Before I buy anything, I ask myself a few questions. Do I want it or do I need it? Can I do without it? Do I already have something that will work instead? What value is this bringing to my life that makes the sacrifice of money/time/space worth the trade?"

–Candice Pombar via the Minimalist Living Facebook page

We talked about filter questions before. Let's touch on them again for the goal of strong armor. The four questions Candice asks are at the core of being an aware shopper. It's the pause that is so important to so many decisions in our life. When we pause and ask ourselves questions, we gain power.

Let's look at each of the four questions individually.

Do I want or do I need it?

This question can help us define why we think we should buy something. Most things are wants, not needs.

Often marketing messages tell you that you need something new when you don't. This can come across like it's for your own safety or in your best interest.

For example, I've noticed this advice given to runners: if you don't frequently replace your running shoes, you are more likely to get injured. This just isn't true for everyone. Some people can run barefoot without getting injured. Others need a certain type of shoe to run injury-free. It depends on the person. Some of us can run miles in worn down shoes. In fact, my feet tend to be happiest in very old, worn shoes. The older my shoes are, the happier my feet are, something I've learned over twenty years of running.

This also goes for bras. I remember buying a bra once, and the bra company had printed on the tag that you need to replace your bras every six months, as if somehow your breasts would suffer in old bras. The truth is, that company wishes you would buy new bras from them every six months. But you do not need all new bras every six months. Some would argue that we do not need bras at all.

Can I do without it?

I love this question because it opens us to creative problem solving. It unlocks magic.

I had these old running shoes that I loved. They were really comfortable and had a black and magenta color scheme I liked.

Then they got a small hole in the top. I thought immediately of throwing them out and buying a new pair. But then I thought "can I do without buying a new pair?" And I thought of two solutions – a piece of tape on the inside of the shoe wouldn't show, and it would let me wear them a little longer. While I was putting the tape on, I thought of how easy and quick it would be to just sew the hole shut.

Asking this filter question got me more mileage out of those running shoes before they finally wore out completely. And I'd purchased those shoes at a thrift store so someone else had already put some miles on them.

Do I already have something that will work instead?

Like the last question, this one sparks creativity. It also forces you to confront novelty and the lack of novelty. Sheer novelty is a powerful force when it comes to buying decisions. It's a thrill. The novelty of a new thing wears off quickly though. This question makes you think of things that your brain might be labeling as "boring," but will do the trick.

Think of what you already have that will function just as well as the new thing you are considering buying. That will be enough to have you recognizing the attractive glow of the novel and acknowledging that it is the main emotion motivating you to consider the purchase.

What value is this bringing to my life that makes the sacrifice of money, time, and space worth the trade?

This powerful question forces you to confront true value. And opportunity cost. There's a "no" behind every yes. If you say "yes" to this purchase, what are you saying "no" to? And don't be fooled – there is always a "no," whether it means you'll be going further into credit card debt or crowding out other items in your closet.

A variation on this question is, "what will I get rid of if I purchase this item?" It helps to gauge the true value of a prospective purchase by deciding, pre-purchase, what will go "out."

How do you live free in a world that wants to clutter you up?

"One: Do I NEED this? Two: If yes, how did I live so long without it? Three: If I WANT it, can I just appreciate its beauty/charm and put it back on the shelf?"

–Ellen Rassiger via the Minimalist Living Facebook Page

Ellen's questions are similar to Candice's, but they bring their own flavor to the pre-purchase conversation you have with yourself, especially questions two and three. Thinking about how long you lived without an item you think you need, will, at the very least, enhance your gratitude and enjoyment of the purchase should you decide to buy it. I am a big fan of number three because I enjoy window shopping. Window shopping is effectively appreciating the charm of an item and the talent of a boutique's window stylist without cracking your wallet.

Lists

Try this: each time you want to buy something, write it down instead. You can buy it later. For now, put it on a list. You can make your list online or offline. Make one big list or subdivide it into categories.

I have a list called "For Purchase Consideration" using Google Keep. Sometimes I see a cool product advertised on Instagram, I think of an item that might improve some aspect of my life, or I see something that would make a good gift. When that happens, I put the item and any relevant links and research on my list.

I started my list when I was living in Ukraine. There, it's not as easy as it is in the U.S. to get things by post. Shopping online – or in person – took more effort with the language barrier. If I wanted to order something, I had to be really motivated and patient. The list proved to be a great delay tactic that resulted in buying less. There was time for the initial lust to cool off. There was time to find a creative solution from what I already owned. There was time to change my mind.

Having the list makes me feel calm and reassured that if I want to remember how to get something I thought was cool, I can reference my list. I don't lose the idea. If you implement your own list, I recommend waiting at least a week, if not a couple of months, before making the final purchase decision.

Limits

Limits, constraints, boundaries, lines in the sand. Whatever you call them, they're your friend when it comes to your anti-impulse purchase armor.

Limits on Time

If you fill your time with fulfilling experiences, you'll have less time for shopping. This creates a natural limit on the time you have for acquisition.

I've come across more than one weight-loss guru who applies this idea to losing weight. The idea is that if your life is full of enriching and fun activities, you won't have to fill your stomach quite as much. It's the same with shopping.

If you find yourself turning to shopping when you're bored, you might need to limit your time spent bored. What else can you do? Make a list of ten meaningful or fun activities that don't require buying anything.

Similarly, if you find yourself turning to emotional shopping to lift your spirits when you're feeling down, place time limits on shopping and make a list of things that bring a smile to your face but don't require shopping.

Limits on Space

If you know your storage space is limited, you're less likely to buy too much stuff. People who live in tiny homes or other small spaces have a built-in limit on how much they can own. Built-in limits can make creating a minimalist life feel easy and natural.

If you don't have built-in limits, try to create them. If you rent a self-storage space, clear it out and do without it. If your closet is too full to push the clothes to one side or easily see what you have, place empty hangers between in-use hangers as spacers. Make a rule for yourself that boxes need to have lids to prevent overfilling them.

We tend to expand into the space available to us. Empty out a closet or two and put a "do not enter" sign on the door temporarily. Make these spaces unavailable until the items in the rest of your home are edited down to what you use and love. Then you can open them up and use the newfound "extra" space in any way you'd like.

Limits on Information

How do you live free in a world that wants to clutter you up?
"I don't watch a lot of TV anymore because of the commercials that say you need this or that. I make myself more aware of the tactics they use as well. I try to spend more time doing other things, like running or hiking with my favorite kids."

–Rachel Matthews via the Minimalist Living Facebook page

What's your diet like? I don't mean the food you eat. I'm talking about your information diet. Do you take in a bunch of sensationalized or one-sided news reporting and a constant stream of ads? Or do you read inspiring and educational books?

I was deeply impressed by the book *Factfulness: Ten Reasons We're Wrong About the World–and Why Things Are Better Than You Think*.[58]

The authors share UN data to show that things in the world are getting better. Not only that, but the book also details how poll after poll showed journalists, politicians, and global business leaders getting it wrong. In other words, the people most of us get our information from—journalists, politicians, and global business leaders – have the wrong facts about the

---

[58] https://www.gapminder.org/factfulness-book/

state of the world. There's a trend of global improvement and has been for the last twenty years.

Our information diet has been full of data that is simply nonexistent or incorrect. Yes, there are lots of bad things happening in the world. There are big problems we must solve. A few things are getting worse in some places. But in most places in the world, things are getting better, thanks to improved healthcare, infrastructure, and educational opportunities. I'm talking about big issues like child mortality, extreme poverty, and gender inequality showing marked improvements over the last twenty years. That sounds too good to be true, but *Factfulness*, uses, well, facts to prove it.

Watching too much news can give us the opposite idea about the world, and it's an idea that just isn't fact-based. The problem isn't that news reports themselves are wrong (although everyone, including journalists, make mistakes). It's that when we ingest bad news stories every day about disease, terrorism, accidents, crime, and weather disasters, we can start to build the wrong big picture of the world in our minds. And it's my opinion that this can lead to chronic low-grade depression we try to heal with impulse shopping and unnecessary consumption.

When we think all day long about a tragedy or disaster we've heard about, we're stealing attention from what is more important – that a lot of things are working in the world and we all have a part to play in figuring out what's working so we can improve it even more.

The global improvements we are making as a species are working better than ever because experts study what *works* and implement more of *that*. We can live more fulfilling lives if we focus on what's working and how to make what's working even better. Yes, it's important to be well-informed, but we can fool ourselves if we only take in some kinds of media. TV news is on a constant cycle meant to keep our attention engaged through scaring the heck out of us and breaking our hearts. It's not the best place to look for accurate and complete data, things going right, or even a well-rounded picture of what's going on in our world.

Make yourself aware of your sources of information. Are you watching a lot of movies, television shows, and online videos? Are you reading a lot of books? Magazines? Your information diet is not just about advertisements, although those are important to limit.

Becoming aware of the information you're taking in can help you make better decisions. Consider what limits on information would be healthy for you to put in place to live with more freedom and joy.

Chapter Eight

So, so busy

When Zina Harrington began her journey to a less busy life, she started with frustration, anger, and "quite a bit of profanity."[59] This was because she'd recently read *The Art of Non-Conformity* by Chris Guillebeau and it made her angry. The book's message that you don't have to live the way others expect you to, that anyone can create a self-designed life through intentional actions, seemed unrealistic to her. It seemed far out of reach. Looking back, she realized her response was mostly about fear.

She overcame her fear and started a blog called Becoming Unbusy. Now she helps parents and families who want their own alternative lifestyle – one that is about being present, doing less, and rejecting the glorification of busy.

Faux Productivity

There's a reason Harrington and others like her want to become less busy. It's because being busy can feel important even when nothing important *to you* is actually getting done. Being busy can be an empty achievement. Feeling busy can fill a need to feel significant but it is a short-lived feeling.

It can seem so important to be doing something rather than nothing, that we start *doing* before we've thought it through. We start doing before we know what is truly important to us. We end up *doing* for the sole reason of being productive. Productivity has great value in our society. We feel we get

---

[59] https://becomingunbusy.com/the-art-of-non-conformity/

our value from doing things – taking action even when it's empty action – even when being busy feels overwhelming and stressful. We become faux productive – we think we have a lot to do – so, so much – but at the end of the day, we haven't done anything that really matters to us.

My message is not mainstream: It's better to do nothing than to do something that doesn't matter. Don't do things that make you dislike your life. Your value comes from your being, not your doing. Don't be faux productive.

It's easy to fall into the faux-productivity track. Checking our phones, answering emails as they come in, opening junk mail, and doing anything that is a distraction from what is most important is faux-productivity.

When I email someone and get a response back instantly, I know it's unlikely they are in a highly productive season of their life. That's because I know they let my email interrupt something else they were doing. Every time you take your focus off your main thing, it takes effort to switch back. Instead of setting up your email to interrupt you, set aside protected time to check and answer your email. Your email and your more important activities will benefit. The exception is if you have a job that requires you to open email as it comes in. You won't be as productive as you could be in that job unless the entire job is answering email.

True productivity results from making space for what is most important. When you have a block of time that is reserved for your most important and meaningful activities, protect it. If you let distractions intrude, you'll be less *truly* productive. You may feel more productive, but you'll get less of the important things done. You'll be living your life on someone else's terms. Experience over stuff is about living your unique life on your terms.

Our Time is Limited

In the last chapter, we talked about limits on time, space, and information when it comes to preventing impulse purchases. Time, of the three, is the only one with an inherent limit that is the same for everyone. Each of us has 24 hours in a day.

This means, again, that for everything we say yes to, we're saying no to something else. So when we say yes to faux productivity, or even just doing things that are somewhat important but not the most important, we're saying no to the most important things in our life. By saying yes to what is of little importance, we're by default saying no to what is most important to us. That's the way time works for all of us.

If we want a life of freedom and purpose, we must always be doing what is most important to us at any given moment. And I want to clarify that if we're doing something for someone else, that act of giving can, of course, be the most important thing in our lives. It's not always, but it can be. By choosing to do what is most important to us, we must, for an interval, ignore everything else. This can feel difficult and even selfish.

My mom puts a lot of her time and energy toward curing brain cancer. She isn't personally a cancer researcher (although she's well informed on the current advances in brain cancer treatment) but she spends a lot of time raising funds for cancer research. After losing her sister Jenny to brain cancer, she made the conscious choice that being part of curing brain cancer by fundraising is one of the most important things in her life. This means to be truly, meaningfully productive, she has to ignore much of the ongoing current other crisis in the world, like what to do about school shootings and sexism and animal cruelty and how pensioners in war-torn Eastern Ukraine will stay warm this winter. That's a lot of things to ignore.

However, she knows that her time is limited and, while it is important to have a sense of what's going on globally, she can't fix all the problems of the world. She's picked one problem to tackle, and that's what she spends most of her problem-fixing time and energy on. This is not to say that other things are not important to her, like her family and her career, but at any given moment she knows what is most important to her, focuses on it, and is therefore saying "no" to the rest.

The Shit Sandwich Problem

Since we have limited time, what will you do to fill it with what matters? How will you avoid faux productivity and create a life you love?

If you want to be happy, your best chance is to do something meaningful and tend to your relationships (as well as your health, which we'll get to in the next chapter).

Your calling is usually where your skills and passions intersect with something the world needs. In other words, find something you love to do, that you're good at, and that helps people in some way.

There's no such thing as a perfect career or calling. As you pursue your purpose, expect some not-so-rosy experiences. In her book *Big Magic*, author Elizabeth Gilbert calls these unenticing aspects of any job, the "shit sandwich." Every career or calling comes with a shit sandwich or two, and you've got to be willing to eat them to stay the course.

If you don't know your purpose in life, congratulations, you're not alone. As I wrote before, all you have to do is explore by taking action. I've discovered that you can't usually think or multiple-choice test your way into knowing your purpose. While there's a place for quiet reflection and meditation on finding your purpose, you also have to get out there and try things and talk to people who are doing what you might want to be doing. Try things out and see if you feel energized and excited, or whatever your desired emotions are. Also, look out for the shit sandwiches – present in every vocation – and ask yourself if you're willing to eat the particular ones that come with the line of work you're exploring. (I've discovered that when you talk to people in any given field, the shit sandwiches usually come up right away as long as they aren't in active recruitment mode. If they don't tell you right away, ask what the pros and cons of the job are. The cons are the shit sandwiches.)

Filter Questions for Your Schedule

Integrity is doing what you say you're going to do.

Rather than dragging yourself dutifully to fulfil an obligation you really don't want to fulfil, it's so much more joyful to think carefully before you say yes to anything. Then, when people ask you to do things, although they might be disappointed when and if you say no, they will also trust you more. They will appreciate your strength of character when you say no, because they will experience your "yes," as something more wholehearted and true than if you're a person who says "yes" when they aren't sure if they can fulfil something or just to get the asker off their back.

To help you think carefully before you make a commitment that you don't truly want to fulfil, ask yourself:

- Does this event or meeting meet my needs?
- Does this commitment serve my purpose?
- If I say yes to this, what am I saying no to?
- If I say yes to this, would it be the most important thing I could be doing with my time?

Consider carefully so you can make your "yes," a wholehearted "yes."

You may need to say "no" more so you can have margin to align your life with what you really want. This goes against the common advice to say "yes" to as many opportunities as possible. There are seasons of life to say "yes" to everything, but they are usually short-lived.

Focus on What You're Creating

No matter how kind you are when you honestly give your "no," some people will see you in a negative light, like in Alice Sandilands' example where she gives the words "lazy" or "uninvested" as examples of how people might see her. She knows that not feeling stressed or overwhelmed is what matters. If other people are thinking judgmental thoughts about you – that's their business. Let people be responsible for their own feelings.

Your responsibility is to what you are bringing into the world. I felt this deeply when giving birth to my second child. I was in a private hospital in Kyiv, Ukraine, and for some reason – maybe the hormones coursing through my body – I felt concerned about other people's needs. No one was asking me for help, but I was taking on responsibility for their needs anyway. For example, I worried that my doctor would resent staying late into the night to deliver the baby. I worried that my husband would be tired if the labor took a long time and he stayed awake with me. I worried the orderlies would be inconvenienced by cleaning up the soiled bed sheets. I worried that my doula would skip her dinner and be hungry.

Even as contractions gripped my whole body I had these overwhelming concerns about what other people were going through. I knew everyone there – my husband, my doula, the doctors, and nurses – were there to support me. My job was to have the baby. But I kept having intrusive concerns about what other people were thinking and feeling.

My baby didn't come until I was able to let go of everything but the matter at hand – bringing a new child into the world in the way that only I knew how. The nurses tried to tell me how to push the baby out, but they were wrong. At one point, I shouted "stop telling me what to do!" I knew what to do, and I was doing it. All I needed was their support and attentive silence. They thought they were right, and so they didn't stop coaching me. I had to tune them out.

Doing it my unique way delivered my sweet baby boy into my arms in the perfect way. I had to stop worrying about what they thought and what they were telling me. I listened to my own inner wisdom which was more well-informed than theirs. As an over-prepared, research-obsessed learner, I've poured years into my own medical and childbirth self-education. I'm not a doctor or a nurse, but I knew much more about *that* childbirth *as it related to my own body and baby in that present, particular moment* than my attending medical team did. I could trust myself.

It was a big leap for me, a steppingstone of growth that felt very spiritual: there's a lot to let go of if you want to enjoy a beautiful birthing. You can't worry too much about what other people think, feel, and say while you're having a baby. You can't worry too much about what other people think, feel, and say while you're doing any work that really matters.

Chapter Nine

The Happiness Essentials

I met a new friend who seemed quite shy. I thought maybe she was risk averse. As I got to know her, I realized that was not the case. One day she pulled up to my house on a new motorcycle. I'm not sure what kind it was – I know very little about motorcycles – maybe a Kawasaki Ninja. It looked really cool. It turns out, owning a motorcycle was a bucket list item for her. She'd been quietly taking motorcycle driving lessons and getting the special license needed to operate one. I had no idea until I saw the motorcycle in the driveway.

Sometime later I attended her wedding. Everyone was invited to stand up and say a few words, so I stood up to toast the bride and groom. I decided to share the above little anecdote to illustrate how badass she was. She seemed like a quiet and reserved person, but she was also a bit of a daredevil with this cool motorcycle. While the room seemed happy with my toast, the bride and groom didn't respond with the big smiles I expected. Instead, they looked a little worried.

After everyone gave their toasts I was chatting with the bride and groom. I asked if I'd said something wrong during my toast. They cringed slightly as they told me that the bride's status as a motorcycle rider was actually a secret. She had some relatives present at the wedding who told her they'd disinherit her if she were to ride a motorcycle.

My heart dropped into my stomach. I had no idea that the motorcycle was a secret. I gave the bride and groom my best wishes and hopes that they would not be disinherited because of my toast.

I thought, why did I even have to give a toast? I didn't have to say a single word. Now I've potentially ruined this young couple's future? I mean, I don't know how big this inheritance is. I wonder how badly I've screwed up. I should just go back to being a shy person who doesn't talk much.

Then I thought, Oh well. There is no way I could have known about the disinheritance thing. Everyone makes mistakes. I was doing my best to be part of a festive celebration. I tried to put the error from my mind and have a good time dancing and eating cake.

Later that evening I met the bride's aunt and uncle - the ones who had apparently threatened to disinherit her if she rode a motorcycle. We bumped into each other in the hallway of the hotel that most of the wedding guests were staying in.

They both gave me a warm smile. "It was nice to meet you," said the uncle.

"And how kind of you to give such a lovely toast," said the aunt.

"Unfortunately, we couldn't hear it," said the uncle.

"The sound system must not have been working," said the aunt.

"We caught some of it, but not all of it," said the uncle.

"Too bad we couldn't hear most of it," said the aunt. They shrugged politely and went on their way.

The Happiness Puzzle

I'm proof that even if you give a bad wedding toast, you can still be happy. Happiness requires being able to move on from mistakes. When I stopped taking myself so seriously, I got a lot happier. I still take myself pretty seriously, as you have probably figured out by reading this book, but I'm a lot better than I used to be.

Besides taking your thoughts and mistakes not-so-seriously, happiness requires finding your own *meaning*, as we discussed in Chapter Three. While self-help authors agree that a meaningful, or purpose-driven life will result in feelings of happiness, contentment, and satisfaction, some researchers assert that there are additional pieces to the happiness puzzle.

In a previously quoted article,[60] John M. Grohol writes, "Relationships are a key factor in long term happiness. While research has demonstrated that this effect is strongest for married people, other research has shown that strong social connections with others are important to our own happiness. The more of these you have, generally, the happier you will be."

George Vaillant, who directed over 30 years of a 75-year longitudinal study called the Grant Study, concluded that "warmth of relationships throughout life has the greatest positive impact on 'life satisfaction'" and, "Happiness is love."[61]

Forbes senior contributor George Brandt analyzed the Grant Study and three other happiness surveys and concluded, "Happiness comes from choosing to be happy with whatever

---

[60] https://psychcentral.com/blog/5-reliable-findings-from-happiness-research/

[61] https://en.wikipedia.org/wiki/Grant_Study

you do, strengthening your closest relationships and taking care of yourself physically, financially and emotionally."[62]

Warm Relationships

Close friendships make us happier. So how do you attract wonderful people into your life?

First of all, be grateful for the people who are already in your life instead of focusing on their flaws. Yes, they probably do have flaws, and big ones, but everyone is trying their best – and that is something to admire about a person and to be grateful for.

Close friendships are formed out of emotional vulnerability coupled with self-reliance. In other words, I find that my friends want to know what's going on with me, in my heart of hearts, – my authentic self – but they also seem to appreciate that I'm strong, resilient, whole, and independent. Vulnerability plus independence seem to be a magnetic duo.

How do you live free in a world that wants to clutter you up?
"Put down/shut off your devices and live in the moment! The less advertisements I see, the less I want to buy/consume. Also, the more I am able to enjoy people in my company, the more I realize it is truly who you have in life, not what - that matters."

–Sonya Ryan via the Minimalist Living Facebook page

Experimenting with Social Norms

There's so much to learn about communication that can help our relationships. It's an endlessly fascinating topic to me. I

---

[62] https://www.forbes.com/sites/georgebradt/2015/05/27/the-secret-of-happiness-revealed-by-harvard-study/#401f76306786

took a class at Meredith College called Communication 101. It was team-taught by two excellent professors. We learned about how most of our communication is nonverbal. A big part of nonverbal communication is abiding – or not abiding – by cultural social norms. There are so many social norms we follow without even realizing it.

One of the assignments for the class was to get out in the real world, break a small social norm, and report back on the experience. This was terrifying to me, so I decided to go big to get over my fear. I would break the social norm that says we do not insert our fingers into our noses in public.

I planted two friends in a Ben and Jerry's ice cream shop near campus. Fifteen minutes later, I walked into the shop with my left index finger up my nose. I kept it there while I ordered a pint of mint chocolate ice cream to go, paid for my order, and I walked out of the shop with my pint.

Apparently after I left the shop, the two ice cream servers behind the counter broke out laughing. But they'd been very polite to me and held in their reactions while I was in the store.

The moral of this story is that nothing terrible happened to me even though I did something disgusting. Afterwards, I became more confident socially. I understood that social dynamics are something to be played with and enjoyed. I was empowered to bend unspoken rules at my choosing, although I have never again done the finger up the nose thing. That's just gross.

Facing fears we have about breaking small social norms can help us feel more comfortable when it comes to meeting people, making friends, and being authentic. I recently heard someone suggest that another way to do this is to ask for discounts everywhere. You really are forced not to worry so much about what people think about you if you ask for a discount for no reason every time you buy something. And you may be surprised how often you get discounts. Of course, this varies depending on what culture you are in. As I write this, I'm in the country of Jordan, where simply asking the price of an item, or saying "that seems like a lot," about the price, can win you a discount.

The point is to question what makes us uncomfortable and why. Is there a reward, something beautiful and freeing to learn about yourself just beyond the edge of your comfort zone?

Listening

An excellent way to attract wonderful relationships in your life is to listen. My sister says that people would rather you be interested than interesting. So true.

Early in my adult life I took this sort of advice to heart and asked lots of questions. I got good at asking my friends questions, but I made a mistake – I didn't always listen to the answers. Once my friend called me on it, saying something like "You ask questions but don't always listen to the answers," and it kind of hurt because I wasn't aware that I was doing that. But I realized she was right.

Since then, I try to ask questions and listen to the answers. A good listener is a rare thing. It's such a good feeling to have a conversation in which I feel deeply heard. Often I didn't even realize how much I had to say on a topic until I'm in conversation with a really good listener.

If you want to be a good listener, start with genuine curiosity and some good, simple, questions. You don't have to get really creative with your questions. In fact, the simpler the better. I find a great starting question is "what's on your mind?" and then basically all you have to ask as a follow up is something like "what else?" or "Is there more?" or "Is there anything else there?"

And it's amazing how often yes, there is more, much more, there. And to offer a listening ear to the "much more" is a rare gift.

I used to hate small talk. Then one day I realized the quality of my small talk was my responsibility. Small talk is an essential part of meeting new people, networking, and early friendship. I hated it because I was asking questions that I wasn't truly curious about. I was asking questions I thought I should ask. I wasn't checking in with myself at all before asking small-talk type questions like "where are you from?" Sometimes I am not very curious about where someone is from. Now my small talk is entirely driven by genuine curiosity. It's still small. I don't ask someone their most cherished life goal, at least not right out of the gate. I start with curiosity and see where it takes us.

One of my best friends, Kimberly, taught me the gift of deep listening. It's a natural talent for her, maybe because she is a middle sibling in a large family and she has a lot of sisters. What I've learned from her about listening could be a book on its own, but the three main things are:

1. Presence. When Kimberly is there, she's there. She's not checking her phone or worrying about what else is going on. She's fully present. She shows that by looking at you and nothing else.

2. Questions. Kimberly is very curious and good at coming up with simple and salient questions. She's also highly sensitive and aware of how people are feeling so she knows when to back off.

3. True Understanding. It can be hard to listen deeply when someone is telling you something that is emotionally distressing. There's a tendency to distance ourselves or bring in our own experience right away. And while it can be nice to hear the other person's perspective on things, it's even nicer to

know we are clearly understood, to hear our feelings repeated back to us with compassion. There's definitely a time and place for sharing how the listener feels in response, or to share a similar situation that shows they know what the other person is going through. But if you can delay the natural human instinct to bring it back to yourself, you'll be giving a rare gift, one that will likely be deeply appreciated. I have a hard time with this, but on the rare occasions that I am able to be selfless in this way, the outcome is striking. I've experienced people shifting their attitude towards me from cold and aloof to warm and deeply affectionate. I think one reason it's hard to offer this true understanding is often the feelings people share are wrapped in a package that can feel alienating or insulting. Next time someone is expressing their emotions in a way that makes you want to pull away, look at it as an opportunity to give the gift of true understanding.

Practicing Forgiveness

A Course in Miracles says "Do you want a quietness that cannot be disturbed, a gentleness that never can be hurt, a deep, abiding comfort, and a rest so perfect it can never be upset? All this forgiveness offers you, and more. It sparkles in your eyes as you awake, and gives you joy with which to meet the day."

Forgiveness, like gratitude, is a powerful force for freedom. I cannot get enough reminders to practice either gratitude or forgiveness. I can't hear too many sermons on gratitude or forgiveness. Every time I hear advice to forgive, or advice to find something I'm genuinely grateful for, I'm, well, I'm grateful for it.

Forgiveness isn't only for the other person, it's for us. It sets us free. I am someone who holds onto things. They say you write and teach about what you need to hear. For me, that's true. My soul is like a steel trap. I have trouble letting go. It's a tendency, but it doesn't define me. I can still let go even though it's harder for me to let go than it is for others. I think it's a personality thing. Some people have a hard time letting go and others have an easier time.

Taking Care of Your Body

It is essential to honor your body as part of living the experience over stuff lifestyle. How can you live free if your body is not operating at its peak? I'm very passionate about this topic because I see people sacrificing their health for productivity.

It's often a self-deception to think we should sacrifice our health for anything. In the long-term, it's really just damaging the instrument we play our music on. Our music is what we have to give to the world, and if you're damaging the instrument in an effort to keep making music, that it's a cycle that won't sustain itself.

We want to create a sustainable, simple experiential life, and taking care of your health comes first. I fear that taking care of your health is either seen as something for health nerds or gym rats or people in industries such as acting, modeling, professional sports, or any health field where you need to look healthy to get clients. That's not true. No matter what your job is, you'll probably do it better and be happier if you're healthier.

We all have aspects of our lifestyle that are non-negotiables for our health. One of mine is getting nine or ten hours of sleep every night. I have felt embarrassed in the past about my above-average sleep needs, and it's taken me decades to not feel bad about it. Getting older helps. When I was younger, I always felt like the "old lady" of the group. I was the person who was always leaving parties early and saying no to going out because I wanted to sleep instead.

What are your health-related non-negotiables?

Environment and Health

We tend to underestimate the affect our environment has on us when it comes to health. I'm talking about the people around us as well as our geographic location. Of course we can improve our health wherever we are. We can exercise and choose healthy food wherever we are. But sometimes we literally need to move (geographically) to get healthier.

I grew up in a North Carolina county where parts were classified as a food desert. That means fresh, nutritious, affordable food was not easily accessible to many residents. In high school many of my classmates subsisted on Mountain Dew, a neon, caffeine-imbued sugar water drink the vending machines offered. The palatable food offered in the cafeteria was nutritionally inadequate. Many of my classmates were obese as a result. You've heard of the freshman fifteen? I had friends who went off to college and experienced the reverse. In a big city with access to fresh, nutritious food, healthier people, and educational opportunities, they lost excess weight and seemed much healthier and happier as a result.

When I lived in Los Angeles, which is a sprawling city, I first lived in Burbank. Burbank does not have the more free-spirited, coastal, wellness-oriented culture the West Side of the city is known for. I longed to move to the West Side. When I finally made the move happen, someone joked with me that everyone who moves to the West Side immediately and automatically loses five pounds. It was a joke based in the truth. With more smoothie shops, salad-based cuisine, yoga pant-based fashion, and beaches to run, walk, and show off on, I easily achieved a healthy, strong body after moving to the West Side.

I'll close this chapter with a story about Shirley Williams, who enhanced her life through physical training. I interviewed Williams for my book *The Wealthy Creative: 24 Successful Artists and Writers Share Their Winning Habits.*

61-year-old artist Shirley Williams had started feeling her energy and strength diminishing about four years earlier, despite a lifetime of eating healthy and exercising. She says, "My studio practice can be physically tough. Keeping my energy up was becoming a challenge. My physical strength was also diminishing and it was getting difficult to move oversized canvases around the studio."

She could have slowed down, assuming that there was nothing she could do about her decreasing stamina. Instead, she shares, "I decided to get serious and began working intensely with a personal trainer three days a week. He trains me hard with weights, kickboxing, and something called plyometrics, a form of explosive cardio. On alternate days, I either speed-walk or do Pilates. Now at 61, I can honestly say I'm in the best physical condition of my life. Exercise and diet make me feel young, strong, energetic, and ambitious. I can now actually see myself working to 100!"

Chapter Ten

Reminding Yourself What Matters

I once worked for someone who would openly pick his nose during meetings. He wouldn't usually do it during meetings with just the two of us, but during round-table-style meetings with the team.

This was different than the time I walked into the ice cream shop with my finger up my nose as part of an experiment for Communication 101. That was a one-time thing and I was aware that it was rude and that I'd never do such a thing again.

Imagine you're sitting at a conference table Monday morning and the boss is digging for a booger while everyone discusses their priorities for the week.

The behavior disgusted and distracted me. I would sit there, shocked, thinking is anyone else seeing this? Am I the only one who got the memo that one is to clean one's nose in private? Also, once that booger finally emerges, where will it go? How are we supposed to focus right now?

I really didn't know how to handle it. I didn't want to risk my job by saying anything to him. I didn't want to offend him. But I knew that more likely than giving offense was the likelihood that *he wouldn't change the behavior.* This I knew from observing his managerial style. He wasn't open to feedback from employees and rarely listened to my other concerns. I had to accept the nose-picking.

In the grand scheme of things, the nose-picking wasn't a big deal. It was a small bad habit expressed by an otherwise good person. A person doing their best. Distracting as it was, it didn't matter *that* much. I needed to remind myself what really mattered.

As an addendum, I later observed that public nose picking isn't taboo in many cultures. I've now traveled through enough airports to have seen a lot of it. It still bothers me, but I tell myself my reaction is a product of my cultural norms and values. I'm just better than them. Just kidding. I remind myself what really matters. Which is usually getting through security, getting to the next gate, washing my hands at some point, and traveling on to the next destination and grand cultural learning experience.

This chapter is about reminding yourself what really matters to *you*. Because when it comes right down to it, no one else is in your head. You have to be your own best friend. You need to remind yourself of the stuff that really matters, or you will, like the younger me, get distracted by what doesn't matter. Annoyingly public nose-picking doesn't matter that much.

It took me some time to learn that my life is so much happier when I don't let small stuff annoy me. When I was a teenager, someone gave me a book called *Don't Sweat the Small Stuff... and It's All Small Stuff*,[63] and it *still* took me a long time to learn this lesson. I'm still learning it.

The way I enjoy dealing with small annoyances is by focusing on what really does matter. The big things. My family, friends, health, and all the gifts that come with life.

---

[63] https://amzn.to/2m2azrz

How do you live free in a world that wants to clutter you up?
"Remind myself daily what truly makes me happy and give myself permission to walk to a different beat, which is a very refreshing feeling!"

–Dianne Ludington via the Minimalist Living Facebook page

So much of living free is about reminding yourself what matters. Over and over. It's easy to forget the wonderful things in our lives because we humans have a cognitive bias towards negativity. We evolved this way to keep our hides alive. And while we still need to think about avoiding danger, there's no need to overthink it. Overthinking – obsessive, ruminant, unhelpful thinking– can be disrupted by reminding yourself what matters.

We need to stay inspired and make small ongoing adjustments as we live the experience over stuff life. We need to remind ourselves what matters over and over. We can do this by connecting with like-minded people as well as through daily spiritual and gratitude practices.

Finding Other Simple Living Enthusiasts

How do you live free in a world that wants to clutter you up?
"Place relationships and experiences above material objects. Surround yourself with likeminded individuals."

–Louisa Wargo via the Minimalist Living Facebook page

To enjoy the experience over stuff lifestyle, it helps to not only have quality friends and great relationships, but to have people in your life who are on the same page as you when it comes to simplifying your life and focusing on experiences and relationships.

You may be great at making friends and nurturing your relationships. But do your friends value experiences over stuff? Variety of opinion and diversity of lifestyle are wonderful and can make your relationships richer. But it does help to have at least some people in your life who are also trying to focus on relationships and experiences.

You can start with reading in online groups, like my own Minimalist Living page on Facebook (Facebook.com/mnmlstlvng) for encouragement. Locally, you can look for people, clubs, communities, and organizations that emphasize sustainable, thrifty, frugal, or simple living and groups that get together and do the things you enjoy doing. Many people find that if they replace their weekend social shopping time with weekend social outdoor time, everything gets a boost, from bank accounts to fitness to the quality of relationships.

I used to shop with friends. But now I rarely make shopping the focus of my social life. I much prefer to spend time with friends hiking or enjoying a meal or sitting on the beach. There's something about seeing a beautiful sunset or field of flowers reflected in a friend's eyes. It's beautiful and soul-filling. And it's not hard to get outside with friends – and it's usually free or very affordable.

My partner and I have a habit of saying "happy sunset" to each other after seeing a particularly beautiful sunset, or even just to mark the coming twilight, to let each other know that another day has passed. Yes, it's really corny, but we don't care. We'd rather be corny then let small moments that hold beauty get away from us. For us it's the moments that matter.

How do you live free in a world that wants to clutter you up?
"Remind yourself that you are the one who decides if you really need something, and never forget that what really matters in life are moments."

−Pia Etchegoimberry via the Minimalist Living Facebook page

Spirituality

Spirituality is hard to define. Wikipedia says, "Modern usages tend to refer to a subjective experience of a sacred dimensions and the 'deepest values and meanings by which people live.'"[64]

A daily spiritual practice will look different from person to person and may vary from day to day. It may be as simple as taking a moment for loving self-care, lighting a candle, or taking a hot bath. It could include praying, reading scripture or inspiring material, or meditation. It could be anything you do with focus and loving intention. It could be time spent contemplating the mysteries of the universe or listening to really good song lyrics.

In a way, this entire book has been about valuing the health of your spirit over material things. But it is worth emphasizing here that a daily spiritual practice is a good thing. According to the Wikipedia article referenced earlier, "Various studies (most originating from North America) have reported a positive correlation between spirituality and mental well-being in both healthy people and those encountering a range of physical illnesses or psychological disorders."[65]

I think bringing spiritual practices into your life routinely can prepare you to have occasional peak experiences of spiritual ecstasy.

---

[64] https://en.wikipedia.org/wiki/Spirituality

[65] https://en.wikipedia.org/wiki/Spirituality#Health_and_well-being

Garden of the Gods

My dad wrote me a beautiful letter for my thirteenth birthday. I lost it when my house burned down, but I remember some of what it contained. He wrote that life is full of things that are difficult and painful. But it's also full of wonderful things, for example chocolate, and back rubs, and sunsets. My dad says he feels the most spiritually connected when he is outside in nature. I feel that way too. I am lucky that growing up we enjoyed lots of outdoor time camping and hiking as a family.

Back in 2012 I flew to Colorado Springs, Colorado to see my brother Steven graduate from the Air Force Academy. After a long ceremony during which President Barack Obama personally congratulated each and every graduating cadet, my family and I took some time to visit with each other and see the sites. We drove to an overlook and got out of the car. The place was Garden of the Gods, and it is a registered National Natural Landmark. I couldn't believe it. It was one of the most beautiful places I had ever seen and felt. I was struck with wonder, and tears came to my eyes. I let myself cry and laugh with pure joy that such a beautiful, majestic, and special-feeling place existed. My siblings looked at me like I was a little crazy, but when I looked at my dad, he understood. He was crying and smiling too.

Gratitude

Over and over we are told by sages to count our blessings. And research backs it up, too. Happiness researcher Shawn Achor uses gratitude exercises to help people rewire their brains to become happier.[66] He tells audiences to think of three events they are grateful for that happened over the last 24 hours.

---

[66] https://www.shawnellis.com/21-day-happiness-challenge/

Experience Over Stuff

If you want to go deeper in your practice of gratitude, write down at least one gratitude in detail daily. Include why, specifically you are grateful for the thing today.

For example, almost every day I'm grateful for my cup of coffee or tea. But the reasons vary. Today it might be, "because it smells so good and it warmed me up on this cold morning." Tomorrow it might be, "because it gives me energy after a night of being awake with the baby." The lush details of your gratitude provide texture your mind can grip; they let you hold onto the good thing for a little longer. Paint your gratitude with a detailed brush.

In addition to the things you are grateful for, acknowledge positive experiences and events too.

After all, if you follow the advice in this book, you'll have more experiences to be grateful for than things to be grateful for.

And while I know not every experience will be easy and fun, it's my hope that many of them will be joyful. I hope that choosing experience over stuff will bring you a life of meaning and bliss beyond your wildest dreams.

THANK YOU

Thank you for reading *Experience Over Stuff*. If you liked this book, please leave a review on its Amazon page. As an independently published work, this book's success depends in large part on reviews from people like you.

ACKNOWLEDGEMENTS

I am grateful for all the support I have received from family and friends to write *Experience Over Stuff*.

Thank you so much to members of the Minimalist Living page on Facebook for their comments and suggestions about living an experience over stuff life.

I appreciate my mom, Maria Parker, for editing this book, and my dad, Jim Parker, for recommending her excellent editorial skills. I'm really lucky in the parent department.

RESOURCES

I mentioned a number of good books in this book. For a list of these books with clickable links to their Amazon listings, visit:

https://simplelivingtoolkit.com/blog/experiencebooks

While you're there, please sign up for the free 3-Day Decluttering Challenge at the bottom of the page.

APPENDIX

How do you live free in a world that wants to clutter you up?

Responses via the Minimalist Living Facebook page retrieved September 13, 2019.

See screenshots here:

Minimalist Living
Published by Genevieve Parker Hill · November 24, 2017

How do you live FREE in a world that wants to clutter you up? Please answer in 1 sentence. I'm doing a little research for my writing 😊 Thanks for the help.

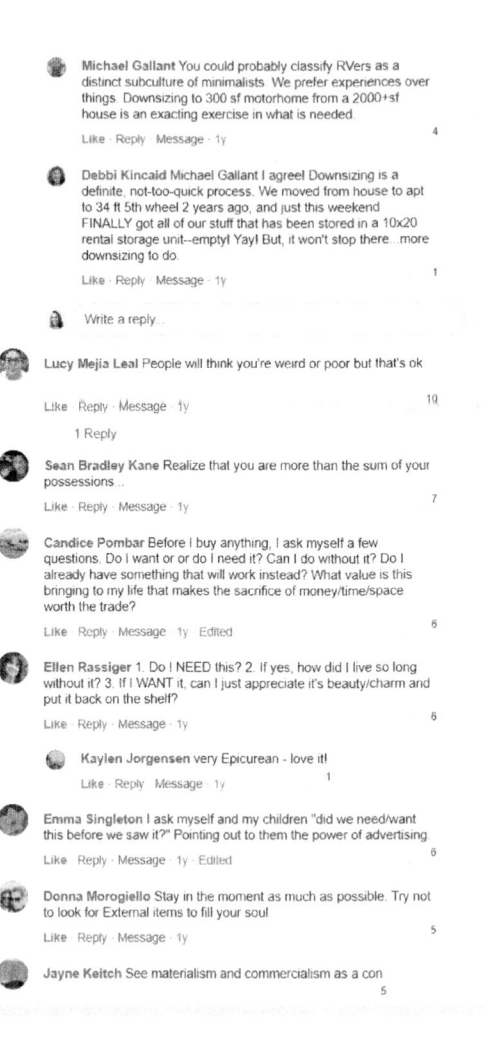

Parker Hill

Michael Gallant You could probably classify RVers as a distinct subculture of minimalists. We prefer experiences over things. Downsizing to 300 sf motorhome from a 2000+sf house is an exacting exercise in what is needed.

Like · Reply · Message · 1y   4

Debbi Kincaid Michael Gallant I agree! Downsizing is a definite, not-too-quick process. We moved from house to apt to 34 ft 5th wheel 2 years ago, and just this weekend FINALLY got all of our stuff that has been stored in a 10x20 rental storage unit--empty! Yay! But, it won't stop there....more downsizing to do.

Like · Reply · Message · 1y   1

Write a reply...

Lucy Mejia Leal People will think you're weird or poor but that's ok

Like · Reply · Message · 1y   10

1 Reply

Sean Bradley Kane Realize that you are more than the sum of your possessions...

Like · Reply · Message · 1y   7

Candice Pombar Before I buy anything, I ask myself a few questions. Do I want or or do I need it? Can I do without it? Do I already have something that will work instead? What value is this bringing to my life that makes the sacrifice of money/time/space worth the trade?

Like · Reply · Message · 1y · Edited   6

Ellen Rassiger 1. Do I NEED this? 2. If yes, how did I live so long without it? 3. If I WANT it, can I just appreciate it's beauty/charm and put it back on the shelf?

Like · Reply · Message · 1y   6

Kaylen Jorgensen very Epicurean - love it!

Like · Reply · Message · 1y   1

Emma Singleton I ask myself and my children "did we need/want this before we saw it?" Pointing out to them the power of advertising.

Like · Reply · Message · 1y · Edited   6

Donna Morogiello Stay in the moment as much as possible. Try not to look for External items to fill your soul

Like · Reply · Message · 1y   5

Jayne Keitch See materialism and commercialism as a con

5

Experience Over Stuff

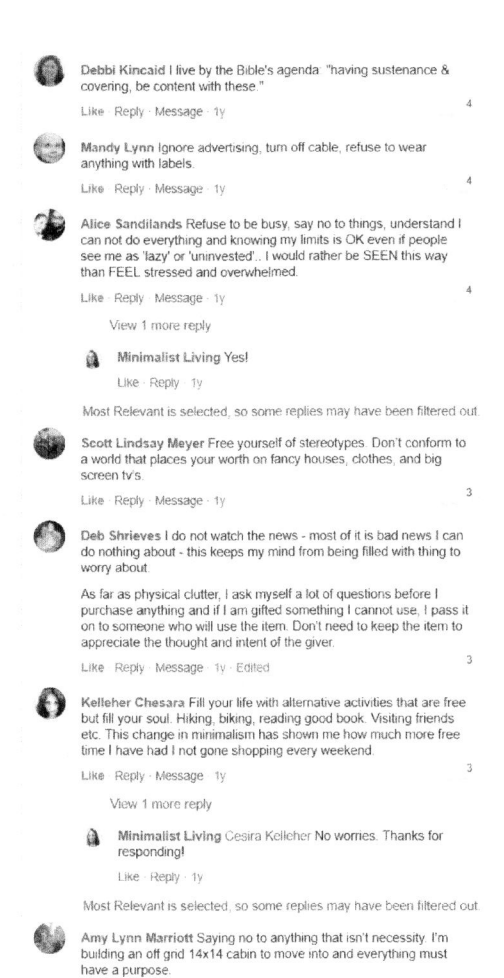

Debbi Kincaid I live by the Bible's agenda: "having sustenance & covering, be content with these."

Like · Reply · Message · 1y — 4

Mandy Lynn Ignore advertising, turn off cable, refuse to wear anything with labels.

Like · Reply · Message · 1y — 4

Alice Sandilands Refuse to be busy, say no to things, understand I can not do everything and knowing my limits is OK even if people see me as 'lazy' or 'uninvested'.. I would rather be SEEN this way than FEEL stressed and overwhelmed.

Like · Reply · Message · 1y — 4

> View 1 more reply
>
> **Minimalist Living** Yes!
>
> Like · Reply · 1y

Most Relevant is selected, so some replies may have been filtered out.

Scott Lindsay Meyer Free yourself of stereotypes. Don't conform to a world that places your worth on fancy houses, clothes, and big screen tv's.

Like · Reply · Message · 1y — 3

Deb Shrieves I do not watch the news - most of it is bad news I can do nothing about - this keeps my mind from being filled with thing to worry about.

As far as physical clutter, I ask myself a lot of questions before I purchase anything and if I am gifted something I cannot use, I pass it on to someone who will use the item. Don't need to keep the item to appreciate the thought and intent of the giver.

Like · Reply · Message · 1y · Edited — 3

Kelleher Chesara Fill your life with alternative activities that are free but fill your soul. Hiking, biking, reading good book. Visiting friends etc. This change in minimalism has shown me how much more free time I have had I not gone shopping every weekend.

Like · Reply · Message · 1y — 3

> View 1 more reply
>
> **Minimalist Living** Cesira Kelleher No worries. Thanks for responding!
>
> Like · Reply · 1y

Most Relevant is selected, so some replies may have been filtered out.

Amy Lynn Marriott Saying no to anything that isn't necessity. I'm building an off grid 14x14 cabin to move into and everything must have a purpose.

Like · Reply · Message · 1y — 2

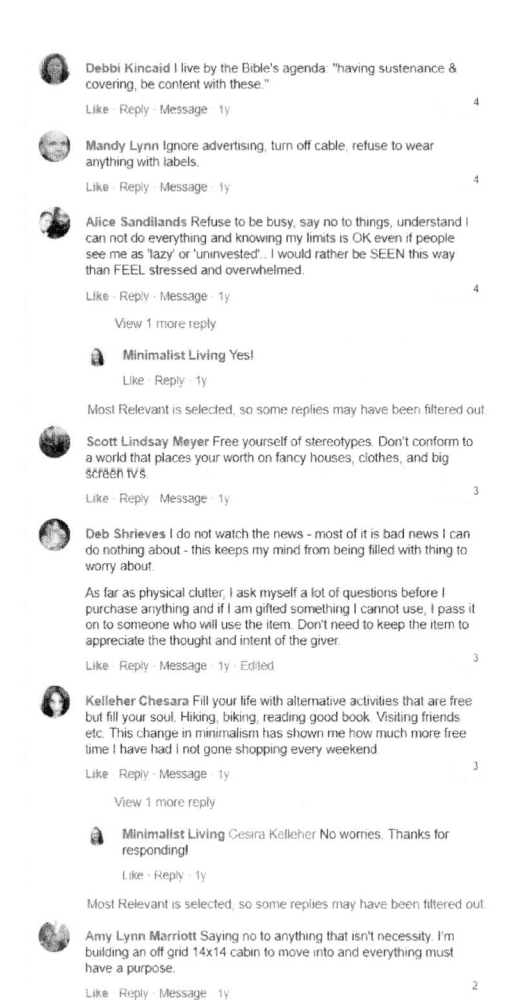

Parker Hill

Debbi Kincaid I live by the Bible's agenda: "having sustenance & covering, be content with these."

Like · Reply · Message · 1y   4

Mandy Lynn Ignore advertising, turn off cable, refuse to wear anything with labels.

Like · Reply · Message · 1y   4

Alice Sandilands Refuse to be busy, say no to things, understand I can not do everything and knowing my limits is OK even if people see me as 'lazy' or 'uninvested'.. I would rather be SEEN this way than FEEL stressed and overwhelmed.

Like · Reply · Message · 1y   4

> View 1 more reply
>
> **Minimalist Living** Yes!
>
> Like · Reply · 1y

Most Relevant is selected, so some replies may have been filtered out.

Scott Lindsay Meyer Free yourself of stereotypes. Don't conform to a world that places your worth on fancy houses, clothes, and big screen tv's.

Like · Reply · Message · 1y   3

Deb Shrieves I do not watch the news - most of it is bad news I can do nothing about - this keeps my mind from being filled with thing to worry about.

As far as physical clutter, I ask myself a lot of questions before I purchase anything and if I am gifted something I cannot use, I pass it on to someone who will use the item. Don't need to keep the item to appreciate the thought and intent of the giver.

Like · Reply · Message · 1y · Edited   3

Kelleher Chesara Fill your life with alternative activities that are free but fill your soul. Hiking, biking, reading good book. Visiting friends etc. This change in minimalism has shown me how much more free time I have had if not gone shopping every weekend.

Like · Reply · Message · 1y   3

> View 1 more reply
>
> **Minimalist Living** Cesira Kelleher No worries. Thanks for responding!
>
> Like · Reply · 1y

Most Relevant is selected, so some replies may have been filtered out.

Amy Lynn Marriott Saying no to anything that isn't necessity. I'm building an off grid 14x14 cabin to move into and everything must have a purpose.

Like · Reply · Message · 1y   2

Experience Over Stuff

---

let live". It has brought me peace to not try to "fix" others who don't want to be fixed.

Like · Reply · Message · 1y · Edited   2

Dede Bolton Pyle Stop feeding consumerism and give some stuff away, sell stuff or just donate what stuff you can to those in need. We don't need a bunch of "stuff" just to be like everyone else. I love not being like everyone else. Im downsizing more and more everyday.

Like · Reply · Message · 1y   3

Sonya Ryan Put down/shut off your devices and live in the moment! The less advertisements I see, the less I want to buy/consume. Also - The more I am able to enjoy people in my company, the more I realize it is truly who you have in life, not what - that matters!

Like · Reply · Message · 1y   2

Amy Beck We spend time outside, in nature! We fill our days with life rather than stay indoors getting bored and feeling the need to fill the void

Like · Reply · Message · 1y   3

Amy Golder A smile is free, a friendship is free, the beach is free, yoga is free, thoughts are free, choose to be different, choose to be you.

Like · Reply · Message · 1y   2

Sam East I spend as much time in the wild as I can

Like · Reply · Message · 1y   3

Rachel Matthews Breeding I don't watch a lot of TV anymore because of the commercials that say you need this or that. I make myself more aware of the tactics they use as well. I try to spend more time doing other things, like running or hiking with my favorite kids.

Like · Reply · Message · 1y   2

Mike Solley I am downsizing into a studio apartment so one day I can live in a tiny house. This helps me not to accumulate too much but keep the items I enjoy

Like · Reply · Message · 1y   2

Stacey Miller Don't step inside a store. Unfortunately, I did succumb to some online shopping for clothes, mainly for my boys, a few things for me. I am weak!

Like · Reply · Message · 1y · Edited   2

1 Reply

Sherry Schnebly If something new comes in, something old gets donated. For example, buy a new shirt donate one that I have. That keeps the clutter way down and helps someone else.

Like · Reply · Message · 1y   2

Cindy Coupe Keep only what you need, organize what you have, don't buy what you don't need, donate things you no longer need and "borrow"/share from friends for events like graduations, etc. instead of buying and storing

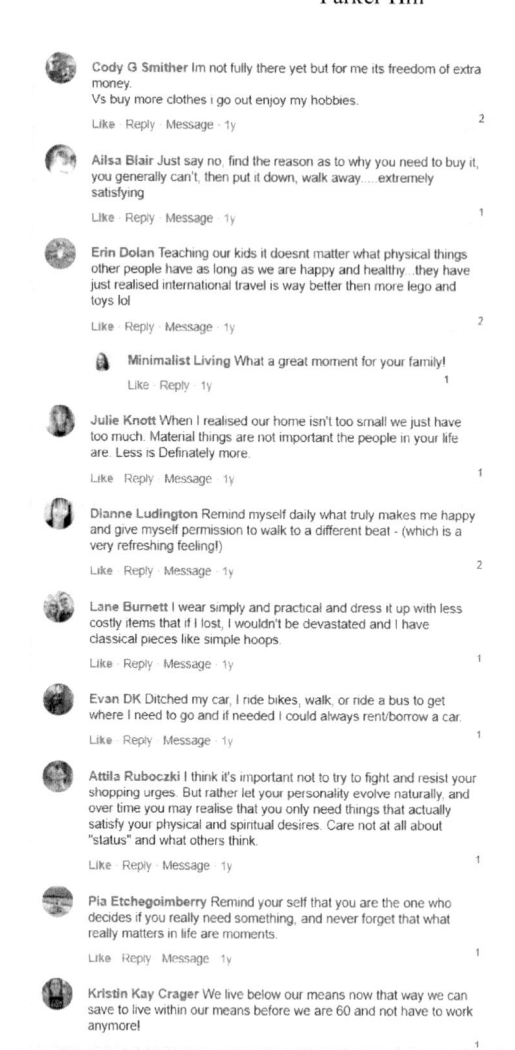

Parker Hill

Cody G Smither Im not fully there yet but for me its freedom of extra money.
Vs buy more clothes i go out enjoy my hobbies.

Like · Reply · Message · 1y   2

Ailsa Blair Just say no, find the reason as to why you need to buy it, you generally can't, then put it down, walk away.....extremely satisfying

Like · Reply · Message · 1y   1

Erin Dolan Teaching our kids it doesnt matter what physical things other people have as long as we are happy and healthy...they have just realised international travel is way better then more lego and toys lol

Like · Reply · Message · 1y   2

> **Minimalist Living** What a great moment for your family!
> Like · Reply · 1y   1

Julie Knott When I realised our home isn't too small we just have too much. Material things are not important the people in your life are. Less is Definately more.

Like · Reply · Message · 1y   1

Dianne Ludington Remind myself daily what truly makes me happy and give myself permission to walk to a different beat - (which is a very refreshing feeling!)

Like · Reply · Message · 1y   2

Lane Burnett I wear simply and practical and dress it up with less costly items that if I lost, I wouldn't be devastated and I have classical pieces like simple hoops.

Like · Reply · Message · 1y   1

Evan DK Ditched my car, I ride bikes, walk, or ride a bus to get where I need to go and if needed I could always rent/borrow a car.

Like · Reply · Message · 1y   1

Attila Ruboczki I think it's important not to try to fight and resist your shopping urges. But rather let your personality evolve naturally, and over time you may realise that you only need things that actually satisfy your physical and spiritual desires. Care not at all about "status" and what others think.

Like · Reply · Message · 1y   1

Pia Etchegoimberry Remind your self that you are the one who decides if you really need something, and never forget that what really matters in life are moments.

Like · Reply · Message · 1y   1

Kristin Kay Crager We live below our means now that way we can save to live within our means before we are 60 and not have to work anymore!

1

Experience Over Stuff

Kristin Kay Crager Purva Poorva We could've afforded a $200K or more larger house, but we choose a simple 3 bedroom for about $150K. We could afford a brand new nice SUV to drive, but we choose to keeps ours that are paid off and dependable. We only buy clothes when need... See More

Like · Reply · Message · 1y   1

Most Relevant is selected, so some replies may have been filtered out

Jermaine Jose By having just the bare essentials and not the consumerism state of mind that the trend is imposing in every advertisement.

Like · Reply · Message · 1y   1

Annelle Woolf Maurer I've been a shopaholic for a long time. Finally said enough. I stay out of stores and throw catalogs away I have all I need. I only buy minimal consumable items

Like · Reply · Message · 1y   2

Lane Burnett I get rid of anything I don't use.

Like · Reply · Message · 1y   3

Troy Steckelbruck Ask myself if I really need the object or is it a want.

Like · Reply · Message · 1y   3

Sara Pritchard If you can't pack your stuff up and leave that home in a day you are not truelly free

Like · Reply · Message · 1y   3

Melissa Schmidt Let GO of all the things you thought you were supposed to be and just be the YOU, you were meant to be all along ♡

Like · Reply · Message · 1y   2

Molly Anne Faith, obedience, and love.

Like · Reply · Message · 1y   3

Andrew McLean Just sold my house and possessions and making it up as I go along.

Like · Reply · Message · 1y   3

Suzanne Michelle Make good and thoughtful choices of what you want more of, things or memories.

Like · Reply · Message · 1y   3

Elizabeth Castaneda Let go... of THINGS.
Things in our house is anything that doesn't clasify as a NEED

Like · Reply · Message · 1y · Edited   3

Angel Rose Grammatico Don't measure your worth in material objects.

Like · Reply · Message · 1y   3

Roy MacArthur Know the difference between wants and needs; get what you need and want what you have.

Like · Reply · Message · 1y   3

Parker Hill

Shahsanam AT Don't go shopping unless you need something in particular

Like · Reply · Message · 1y — 3

Diane Burnham Downsize your life wherever you can!

Like · Reply · Message · 1y — 3

Robin Eustice Wilkes Just be happy, not matter what.

Like · Reply · Message · 1y — 2

Lauri Hofmann Chandler Knowing that joy comes from being content with who I am & not what I have.

Like · Reply · Message · 1y — 3

Laura Halleran "Everything you gather is just more that you can lose."

Like · Reply · Message · 1y — 2

Patrick Smith Remember how freeing it is to have space and fewer belongings to care for, then act accordingly

Like · Reply · Message · 1y — 2

Emily Beck Stop buying and doing what isn't helpful, useful, or truly enjoyed!

Like · Reply · Message · 1y — 2

Patrick Singson Travel the world with just a backpack, automatic minimalist.

Like · Reply · Message · 1y — 2

Rachel Willard Don't listen to the comments or judgement of others

Like · Reply · Message · 1y — 2

Michael Marth Live life on your terms and not societies.

Like · Reply · Message · 1y — 2

Kevin Helms I see how some of my other family members live and want no part of it!

Like · Reply · Message · 1y — 2

Armen Ringgo Sukiro In the world full of negativity, stay positive.

Like · Reply · Message · 1y — 2

JJ Moreno I don't "do" Black Friday shopping.

Like · Reply · Message · 1y — 2

Jeanette Sandelin I've stopped buying things since the 1st of October 2015 and for life   Freedom

— 2

Experience Over Stuff

Harvey Rickard If all my stuff can't fit in my car I can't get rid of things.
Like · Reply · Message · 1y — 2

2 Replies

Amy Malley-Fawkes By recognizing that I have everything I 'need'
Like · Reply · Message · 1y — 2

Linda McCausland Loving these answers! I like the quote: Use it up, wear it out, make it do, or do without by Boyd K Packer
Like · Reply · Message · 1y · Edited — 2

Robin Qualmann i remind myself that when I die, it isn't coming with me
Like · Reply · Message · 1y — 2

Rachel Herndon Be realistic and say no in order to be able to say yes to other things
Like · Reply · Message · 1y — 2

Wade Davis You focus on "who is in your life" and not on "what is in your life."
Like · Reply · Message · 1y — 2

hoo.gy You can rent stuff instead of buying them. We are here to help
Like · Reply · Message · 1y — 2

Ryan Kärgel I try to weigh the impact an object has on the human community, rather just myself.
Like · Reply · Message · 1y — 1

Kelley Bean I try to enjoy experiences, not stuff. My memories of living in the moment are reward enough.
Like · Reply · Message · 1y — 1

Paul Evans De-clutter and live a minimalist life is a great idea
Like · Reply · Message · 1y — 1

Jaime Abbas Restorff Time is my most finite resource, I must always be a good steward of my time.
Like · Reply · Message · 1y — 1

Lane Burnett I also will buy something on a good sale if I will use it and it will bring me joy
Like · Reply · Message · 1y — 1

Ari Love De clutter your mind of all excess and you will find it easier to minimize everything else.
Like · Reply · Message · 1y — 1

Stephanie Beverage Dunlap I think ... do I need it? Is it any better that what I got now? And one thing out for one thing in
Like · Reply · Message · 1y — 1

Ena Soto Pacheco Meditation, renewing of my mind!
Like · Reply · Message · 1y — 1

Parker Hill

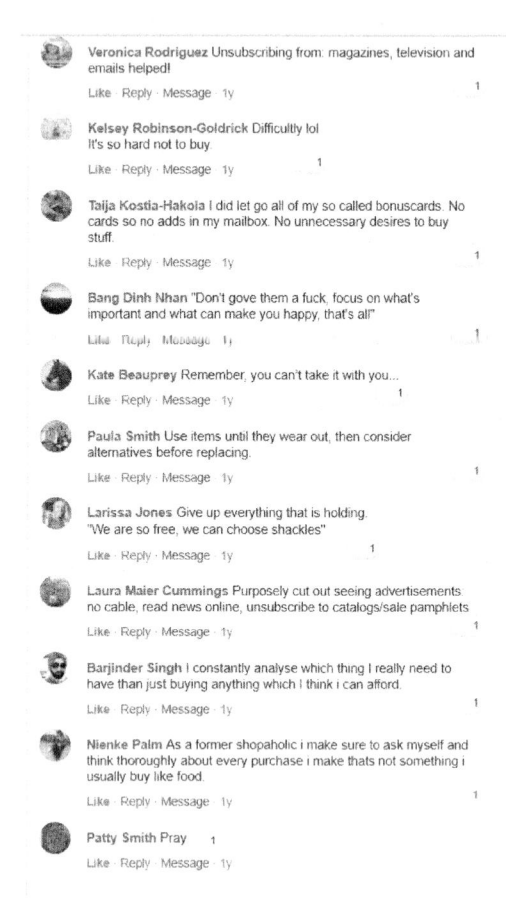

Veronica Rodriguez Unsubscribing from: magazines, television and emails helped!
Like · Reply · Message · 1y

Kelsey Robinson-Goldrick Difficultly lol
It's so hard not to buy.
Like · Reply · Message · 1y

Taija Kostia-Hakola I did let go all of my so called bonuscards. No cards so no adds in my mailbox. No unnecessary desires to buy stuff.
Like · Reply · Message · 1y

Bang Dinh Nhan "Don't gove them a fuck, focus on what's important and what can make you happy, that's all"
Like · Reply · Message · 1y

Kate Beauprey Remember, you can't take it with you....
Like · Reply · Message · 1y

Paula Smith Use items until they wear out, then consider alternatives before replacing.
Like · Reply · Message · 1y

Larissa Jones Give up everything that is holding.
"We are so free, we can choose shackles"
Like · Reply · Message · 1y

Laura Maier Cummings Purposely cut out seeing advertisements. no cable, read news online, unsubscribe to catalogs/sale pamphlets
Like · Reply · Message · 1y

Barjinder Singh I constantly analyse which thing I really need to have than just buying anything which I think i can afford.
Like · Reply · Message · 1y

Nienke Palm As a former shopaholic i make sure to ask myself and think thoroughly about every purchase i make thats not something i usually buy like food.
Like · Reply · Message · 1y

Patty Smith Pray
Like · Reply · Message · 1y

Experience Over Stuff

Steve Grubich "A flood in the basement sure makes it easy to declutter"

...my mom said this earlier this year after a flash flood backed up the sewer line to the family home.... See More

Like · Reply · Message · 1y

Anne Burmeister I feel a full heart when gratefulness journaling, noticing so much I take for granted sometimes that I want to thank God for, get out into nature, and help others.

Like · Reply · Message · 1y

Paula Cook Exchange one thing for another, don't add anything without getting rid of something...eventually you will only own items you absolutely love

Like · Reply · Message · 1y

Carolyn Bostic For myself, my physical disability keeps me close to home. I don't shop online, simply "window-shop".

Like · Reply · Message · 1y

Erin Brewster Fill your days with experiences. Not stuff!

Like · Reply · Message · 1y   3

Betsy Jarosz Don't love anything that won't love you back... less is best

Like · Reply · Message · 1y   2

Alex Gray Discipline to resist the consumer culture

Like · Reply · Message · 1y   2

Diana Spears cut the emotional umbilical cord between you and stuff because the stuff actually has no meaning in it

Like · Reply · Message · 1y   2

Rahel Namba Don't be afraid to reuse, recycle, repurpose, or to throw away.

Like · Reply · Message · 1y   1

Jill Counsell Schuettpelz Ask myself, is this a need or a want

Like · Reply · Message · 1y   1

Sarah Gilbert Say no. Out loud... often. Super liberating once you start.

Like · Reply · Message · 1y   1

Amy Fortune Perry MINIMalism gives us the means to live free.

Like · Reply · Message · 1y   1

Claire Weston With a ton of difficulty/unsuccessfully

Like · Reply · Message · 1y

Mallorie Hurlbert By taking a moment to be mindful of what is truly important in my life.

Like · Reply · Message · 1y

Anita Kedzior If its not practical or beautiful i dont keep or buy it

Sonja Tyson Remind yourself that your actions define you, not your purchases.

Like · Reply · Message · 1y

Monie Fulmer Rowland Every item I own must have an important purpose in my daily life that justifies the prime real estate it is taking up in my life and home.

Like · Reply · Message · 1y

Ungahnah Pathak It's surrounding yourself with like minded people

Like · Reply · Message · 1y

Pierre Bolden Simplify the meaning of normal

Like · Reply · Message · 1y

Tracy White When I shop it's a need not a want .. Avoiding consumerism

Like · Reply · Message · 1y

Shronda Patrick McFarland Be a conscious consumer...stop buying stuff that doesnt add value to your life.

Like · Reply · Message · 1y

Bob Fortune No one is forcing you to do anything. You make your own choices.

Like · Reply · Message · 1y

Danielle Murgida I ignore consumerism.... it's boring and limiting. Minimalism is freedom.

Like · Reply · Message · 1y

Lindsay Morton If you don't love it or have a place for it don't buy it.

Like · Reply · Message · 1y

Rick Majercik Is it a need or a want?? When in doubt, wait a week.

Like · Reply · Message · 1y   1

Nathan Robinson Organize the clutter and attack it 1 problem at a time.

Like · Reply · Message · 1y

Muthu Kumar Awareness when buying, storing n using

Experience Over Stuff

Jackie Hockley If I don't use it, I lose it
Like · Reply · Message · 1y

Martyn Sylvester By being present in the moment
Like · Reply · Message · 1y

Ron Alyn Warner Keep it simple
Like · Reply · Message · 1y

Bow laziness because owning objects is hard work
Like · Reply · Message · 1y

Carly Marie Duce When it doubt chuck it out
Like · Reply · Message · 1y

Brenda Bautista Just say NO!
Like · Reply · Message · 1y

Jennifer Cisewski Start with self care
Like · Reply · Message · 1y

Bree Malone Don't follow the crowd
Like · Reply · Message · 1y

Lesley Olarlu Let it go!
Like · Reply · Message · 1y

Rob Bourguignon Clarity
Like · Reply · Message · 1y

Cindy Lonsinger Find purpose
Like · Reply · Message · 1y

Dave Vanderveen Live within your means
Like · Reply · Message · 1y

Rosemary Curry Stay focused
Like · Reply · Message · 1y

Lola Montgomery Detachment
Like · Reply · Message · 1y

Dave Vanderveen #vanlife
Like · Reply · Message · 1y

Kara Lynne Schwartz .
Like · Reply · Message · 1y

Amy Verlennich 3 words... crazy.simple.good.
Like · Reply · Message · 1y

Swarnab Banerjee Get ur intention right!!
Like · Reply · Message · 1y

Erich Kulibert Meditation